MathFlare

Name: _______________________

Class: __________

Teacher: _______________________

Introduction

As parents and educators, we recognize the pivotal role mathematics plays in shaping a child's academic journey and future success. Yet, the path to mathematical proficiency can often seem daunting, fraught with challenges and complexities. That's where the transformative power of MathFlare Workbooks shine through, illuminating the way forward with clarity, precision, and purpose.

Introducing MathFlare Workbooks – a beacon of guidance, a testament to excellence, and a catalyst for achievement. Crafted with meticulous care and expertise, MathFlare Workbooks stand as paragons of educational excellence, designed to nurture young minds, ignite a passion for learning, and develop a deep-rooted understanding of mathematical concepts.

Picture this: your child eagerly delves into the pages of Mathflare Workbook, greeted by a step-by-step guide illuminated with vivid examples that demystify complex mathematical concepts. With each turn of the page, they embark on a journey of discovery, encountering thoughtfully curated practice questions that reinforce learning and hone problem-solving skills. And when they unveil the answers to those very questions, a sense of accomplishment blossoms within them – a tangible reward for their hard work and dedication.

But MathFlare Workbooks are more than just tools for learning; they are pathways to comprehension, fostering a deep-seated understanding of mathematical concepts through a sequential, logical flow. From fundamental principles to advanced problem-solving strategies, every chapter builds upon the last, ensuring a robust foundation upon which future knowledge can be constructed.

As parents, we yearn for nothing more than to see our children thrive, to witness the spark of inspiration ignited within them as they conquer academic challenges with confidence and poise. MathFlare Workbooks serve as partners in this noble endeavor, offering not just practice questions, but the keys to unlocking a world of opportunity.

And for teachers, MathFlare Workbooks stand as invaluable allies in the quest to cultivate mathematical proficiency in the classroom. With answers readily available, instructors can focus on guiding and nurturing their students, confident in the knowledge that MathFlare Workbooks provide a solid framework upon which to build.

In the pages of MathFlare Workbooks, we find not just the promise of academic excellence, but the seeds of a brighter tomorrow. So let us embrace the power of mathematics, let us champion the journey of learning, and let us pave the way for a generation of young minds poised to shape the world. With MathFlare Workbooks as our guide, the possibilities are infinite, and the future, bright.

Table of Contents

MathFlare
MATH
WORKBOOK
Grade 2
Step by Step Guide
and Essential Practice
with Answers
Addition
Subtraction
Multiplication
Place Value and
Expanded
Notations
Geometry
MathFlare Publishing

MathFlare
MATH
WORKBOOK
Grade 2-3
Step by Step Guide
and Essential Practice
with Answers
Addition
Subtraction
Multiplication
and Division
Place Value and
Expanded
Notations
Geometry
MathFlare Publishing

MathFlare
MATH
WORKBOOK
Grade 3
Step by Step Guide
and Essential Practice
with Answers
Multiplication
and Division
Decimals
Place Value and
Expanded
Notations
Fractions
and Geometry
MathFlare Publishing

MathFlare
MATH
WORKBOOK
Grade 1
Step by Step Guide
and Essential Practice
with Answers
Counting and
Numbers
Addition and
Subtraction
Place Value and
Expanded
Notations
Understanding
Time
MathFlare Publishing

MathFlare
MATH
WORKBOOK
Grade 1-2
Step by Step Guide
and Essential Practice
with Answers
Counting and
Numbers
Addition and
Subtraction
Place Value and
Expanded
Notations
Understanding
Time
MathFlare Publishing

MathFlare
MATH
WORKBOOK
Grade 3-4
Step by Step Guide
and Essential Practice
with Answers
Addition
Subtraction
Multiplication
Division
Place Value and
Expanded
Notations
Fractions
and Geometry
MathFlare Publishing

MathFlare
MATH
WORKBOOK
Grade 4
Step by Step Guide
and Essential Practice
with Answers
Addition
Subtraction
Multiplication
Division
Place Value and
Expanded
Notations
Fractions
and Geometry
MathFlare Publishing

MathFlare
MATH
WORKBOOK
Grade 4-5
Step by Step Guide
and Essential Practice
with Answers
Multiplication
Division
Place Value and
Expanded
Notations
Fractions
and Geometry
Unit
Conversion
MathFlare Publishing

MathFlare
Grade 5
MATH WORKBOOK
Step by Step Guide and Essential Practice with Answers
Multiplication Division
Place Value and Expanded Notations
Fractions and Geometry
Unit Conversion
MathFlare Publishing

MathFlare
Grade 5-6
MATH WORKBOOK
Step by Step Guide and Essential Practice with Answers
Multiplication Division
Place Value and Expanded Notations
Fractions and Geometry
Units and Statistics
MathFlare Publishing

MathFlare
Grade 6
MATH WORKBOOK
Step by Step Guide and Essential Practice with Answers
Integers and Statistics
Arithmetic and Pre-Algebra
Fractions and Geometry
Ratio and Percentage
MathFlare Publishing

MathFlare
Grade 6-7
MATH WORKBOOK
Step by Step Guide and Essential Practice with Answers
Arithmetic and Pre-Algebra
Ratio, Percent Proportion
Geometry
Statistics
MathFlare Publishing

MathFlare
Grade 7
MATH WORKBOOK
Step by Step Guide and Essential Practice with Answers
Pre-Algebra
Ratio, Percent Proportion
Geometry
Statistics
MathFlare Publishing

MathFlare
Grade 7-8
MATH WORKBOOK
Step by Step Guide and Essential Practice with Answers
Pre-Algebra
Ratio, Percent Proportion
Geometry and Cartesian Plane
Statistics
MathFlare Publishing

MathFlare
Grade 8-9
MATH WORKBOOK
Step by Step Guide and Essential Practice with Answers
Pre-Algebra
Ratio, Proportion and Percentage
Linear Equations
Geometry and Cartesian Plane
MathFlare Publishing

MathFlare
Grade 8
MATH WORKBOOK
Step by Step Guide and Essential Practice with Answers
Pre-Algebra
Percentage
Linear Equations
Geometry
MathFlare Publishing

Evaluate Expressions

Evaluating expressions involves substituting given values for variables in an expression and then performing the indicated operations to find the result.

For example: Let's evaluate $4x - 10$, when $x = 3$:

Step 1: Substitute the given value for the variable:

Replace every occurrence of x in the expression $4x - 10$ with the given value, which is 3:

$$= 4(3) - 10$$

Step 2: Perform the operations:

Perform the indicated operations according to the order of operations (PEMDAS - Parentheses, Exponents, Multiplication and Division, Addition and Subtraction):

$$= 4 \times 3 - 10$$

Step 3: Simplify:

Calculate the result:

$$12 - 10 = 2$$

Solving Equations (One Side)

Solving one-step equations involves performing a single operation to isolate the variable and find its value.

Let's solve an equation step by step: $16 + x = 31$

1. Identify the Goal:

    The goal is to isolate the variable x on one side of the equation.

2. **Simplify the Equation**: Combine like terms on both sides of the equation, if necessary.

> The equation is already simplified.

3. **Undo Addition or Subtraction**: If there's addition or subtraction involving the variable, undo it by performing the opposite operation on both sides of the equation.

> Since x is being added to 16, we'll undo this operation by subtracting 16 from both sides of the equation:

$$16 + x - 16 = 31 - 16$$

4. **Isolate the Variable**: Ensure that the variable is alone on one side of the equation.

$$X = 15$$

5. **Check Your Solution**: Substitute the value of x back into the original equation to verify that it satisfies the equation.

$$16 + 15 = 31$$

$$31 = 31$$

The equation is balanced, so the solution.

Equations (Two Sides)

A two-sided equation is an equation where both sides have expressions with variables and constants. The goal when solving a two-sided equation is to find the value of the variable that makes both sides equal.

For example: Let's solve an equation:

$$9 + 8x + 8 = 64 + x + 2$$

- **Combine Like Terms:** Simplify each side of the equation by combining like terms (terms with the same variable or constants).

$$9 + 8x + 8 = 64 + x + 2$$

$$17 + 8x = 66 + x$$

- **Isolate the Variable:** Use inverse operations to isolate the variable on one side of the equation.

subtract x from both sides:

$$17 + 8x - x = 66 + x - x$$

$$17 + 7x = 66$$

subtracting 17 from both sides:

$$17 - 17 + 7x = 66 - 17$$

$$7x = 49$$

divide both sides by 7:

$$\frac{7x}{7} = \frac{49}{7} = x = 7$$

- **Check Solution:** Once you find the solution, substitute it back into the original equation to ensure it makes the equation true.

Substitute $x = 7$ back into the original equation:

$$9 + 8(7) + 8 = 64 + 7 + 2$$

$$9 + 56 + 8 = 64 + 7 + 2$$

$$73 = 73$$

<u>Find Numbers (Verbal Algebra)</u>

Verbal algebra involves translating word problems or verbal statements into algebraic expressions or equations.

For example: The product of the two numbers is 91. One number is six less than the other. What are the numbers?

We're given a verbal description of a problem, and we need to represent it using algebraic symbols and equations.

Let's break down the given problem into algebraic expressions:

- Given that the product of the two numbers is 91, we can write the equation: $xy = 91$
- Also, given that one number is six less than the other, we can write another equation: $x = y - 6$

Now, we can use algebraic techniques to solve the system of equations to find the values of x and y, which represent the two numbers.

$$x(x - 6) = 91$$

1. Solve the equation:

   - Expand the equation:

   $$x^2 - 6x = 91$$

   - Rearrange the equation into standard quadratic form:

   $$x^2 - 6x - 91 = 0$$

   - Factor the quadratic equation:

   $$(x - 13)(x + 7) = 0$$

2. Find the solutions for x.

- From the factored form, we have two possible values for x:

$$x = 13 \text{ or } x = -7$$

3. **Check the validity of the solutions:**

   - Since one number is six less than the other, we discard the negative solution.

   - Therefore, the solution is $x = 13$.

4. **Find the other number:**

   - Substitute $x = 13$ into the expression for the other number:

   Other number $= x - 6 = 13 - 6 = 7$

So, the two numbers are 13 and 7.

Solving Inequalities

Inequalities are mathematical expressions that compare the relative sizes of two values. They are used to express relationships where one quantity is:

- "<" (less than),
- ">" (greater than),
- "<=" (less than or equal to),
- ">=" (greater than or equal to),
- and "≠" (not equal to) another quantity.

For example:

$$y + {-10} \leq {-8}$$

To isolate y, we need to get rid of the constant term -10. Since -10 is being subtracted from y, we can undo this operation by adding 10 to both sides of the inequality:

$$y - 10 + 10 \le -8 + 10$$

$$y \le 2$$

To check the solution:

$$2 - 10 \le -8$$

$$-8 = -8$$

The inequality is true when $y = 2$

Linear Equation

A linear equation is an algebraic equation that represents a straight line when graphed on a coordinate plane. It consists of variables raised to the power of 1 (i.e., no exponents higher than 1) and constant coefficients.

The general form of a linear equation in one variable x is:

$$ax + b = 0$$

Where a and b are constants, and x is the variable.

Let's solve the linear equation:

$$-2x + 9 = 5$$

- **Isolate the variable term:** We want to isolate the term containing x on one side of the equation. To do this, we'll move the constant term to the other side. Subtract 9 from both sides:

$$-2x + 9 - 9 = 5 - 9$$

$$-2x = -4$$

- **Divide by the coefficient of the variable:** To solve for x, divide both sides by the coefficient of x, which is -2:

$$\frac{-2x}{-2} = \frac{-4}{-2}$$

$$x = 2$$

<u>Slop from Two Points</u>

The slope between two points on a Cartesian coordinate system is a measure of the steepness of the line connecting those points. It's calculated by finding the change in the y-coordinates divided by the change in the x-coordinates.

- The coordinates of the first point as $(x_1, y_1) = (2, -30)$.

- The coordinates of the second point as $(x_2, y_2) = (-5, 40)$.

The formula to calculate the slope (m) between two points:

$$\frac{y_2 - y_1}{x_2 - x_1}$$

$$= \frac{40 - (-30)}{-5 - 2} = \frac{70}{-7}$$

$$\text{Slope} = -10$$

Quadratic Equations

A quadratic equation is a polynomial equation of the second degree, meaning it can be written in the form:

$$ax^2 + bx + c = 0$$

where a, b, and c are constants, and x is the variable being solved for. The solutions to a quadratic equation are the values of x that make the equation true.

Now, let's solve the quadratic equation $11x^2 - 1 = 0$ and understand it step by step using quadratic formula.

1. **Identify the coefficients:**

    In the equation $11x^2 - 1 = 0$,

    $$a=11, b=0, \text{ and } c=-1.$$

2. **Apply the quadratic formula:**

    The quadratic formula states that for an equation $ax^2 + bx + c = 0$, the solutions for x are given by:

    $$x = \frac{-b \pm \sqrt{b^2 - 4ac}}{2a}$$

    Plugging in the values a=11, b=0, and c=−1 into the quadratic formula, we get:

    $$x = \frac{-0 \pm \sqrt{0 - 4(11)(-1)}}{2(11)}$$

3. Simplify inside the square root:

$$0^2 - 4(11)(-1) = 0 - (-44) = 44$$

4. Plug in the simplified values:

$$x = \frac{\pm \sqrt{44}}{22}$$

5. Simplify the square root:

Since 44 is not a perfect square, we can write it as $\sqrt[2]{11}$

$$x = \frac{\pm \sqrt[2]{11}}{22}$$

6. Simplify further if possible:

We can simplify $\sqrt[2]{11}$ to $\sqrt{11}$ by canceling out the common factor:

$$x = \frac{\pm \sqrt{11}}{11}$$

7. Final solution:

So, the solutions to the equation are:

$$x = \frac{\sqrt{11}}{11} \text{ and } x = \frac{-\sqrt{11}}{11}$$

or

$$(x = 0.302, \text{ and } x = -0.302)$$

These are the roots of the quadratic equation. They represent the points where the graph of the quadratic equation intersects the x-axis.

Let's solve another equation:

$$-4p^2 + 6p - 6 = 0$$

$$p = \frac{-b \pm \sqrt{b^2 - 4ac}}{2a}$$

where $a = -4$, $b = 6$, and $c = -6$.

Let's plug these values into the quadratic formula:

$$p = \frac{-6 \pm \sqrt{6^2 - 4(-4)(-6)}}{2(-4)}$$

First, let's simplify inside the square root:

$$6^2 - 4(-4)(-6)$$

$$= 36 - 96 = -60$$

So, we have:

$$p = \frac{-6 \pm \sqrt{-60}}{-8}$$

We can simplify the square root of −60 by factoring out −1:

$$\sqrt{-60}$$

$$= \sqrt{-1 \times 60}$$

$$= \sqrt{-1} \times \sqrt{60}$$

$$= i\sqrt{60}$$

So, we have:

$$p = \frac{-6 \pm i\sqrt{60}}{-8}$$

Simplify:

$$\sqrt{60} \text{ to } \sqrt{4 \times 15} = 2\sqrt{15}$$

$$p = \frac{-6 \pm i \times 2\sqrt{15}}{-8}$$

Now, divide both the numerator and denominator by −2 to simplify:

$$p = \frac{3 \pm i\sqrt{15}}{4}$$

So, the solutions to the equation are:

$$p = \frac{3 + i\sqrt{15}}{4} \quad \text{and} \quad p = \frac{3 - i\sqrt{15}}{4}$$

This equation $-4p^2 + 6p - 6 = 0$ has no real solutions.

When a quadratic equation has no real solutions, it means that the solutions are not real numbers, but rather complex numbers. In this case, the solutions involve the imaginary unit i because the discriminant ($b^2 - 4ac$) is negative, which results in taking the square root of a negative number when applying the quadratic formula.

In mathematics, such equations are said to have "no real roots" or "no real solutions." They are also sometimes referred to as having "complex roots" or "complex solutions." Complex numbers include a real part and an imaginary part, and they are often written in the form $a + bi$, where a and b are real numbers and i is the imaginary unit, defined as $i = \sqrt{-1}$.

Let's solve another equation:

$$12x^2 + 6x - 2 = 0$$

$$x = \frac{-b \pm \sqrt{b^2 - 4ac}}{2a}$$

where $a = 12$, $b = 6$, and $c = -2$.

Let's plug these values into the quadratic formula:

$$x = \frac{-6 \pm \sqrt{6^2 - 4(12)(-2)}}{2(12)}$$

First, let's simplify inside the square root:

$$6^2 - 4(12)(-2)$$

$$= 36 - (-96)$$

$$= 36 + 96$$

$$= 132$$

So, we have:

$$x = \frac{-6 \pm \sqrt{132}}{24}$$

Now, let's simplify the square root of 132:

$$x = \frac{-6 \pm \sqrt{4 \times 33}}{24}$$

$$x = \frac{-6 \pm 2\sqrt{33}}{24}$$

$$x = \frac{-6 \pm \sqrt{33}}{12}$$

So, the solutions to the equation are:

$$x = \frac{-6 + \sqrt{33}}{12} \text{ and } x = \frac{-6 - \sqrt{33}}{12}$$

or (x = 0.229, and x = -0.729)

Let's solve a quadratic equation where the right side is a number, instead of 0.

$$-8n^2 + 6n + 30 = 7$$

To solve the equation, we first need to bring all terms to one side to set the equation equal to zero:

$$-8n^2 + 6n + 30 - 7 = 0$$

Simplify:

$$-8n^2 + 6n + 23 = 0$$

Now, to solve for n, we can use the quadratic formula:

$$n = \frac{-b \pm \sqrt{b^2 - 4ac}}{2a}$$

where $a = -8$, $b = 6$, and $c = 23$.

Plugging these values into the formula, we get:

$$n = \frac{-6 \pm \sqrt{6^2 - 4(-8)(23)}}{2(-8)}$$

$$n = \frac{-6 \pm \sqrt{36 + 736}}{-16}$$

$$n = \frac{-6 \pm \sqrt{772}}{-16}$$

Now, let's simplify the square root of 772. We can factor out 4:

$$\sqrt{772} = \sqrt{4 \times 193} = 2\sqrt{193}$$

So, our equation becomes:

$$n = \frac{-6 \pm 2\sqrt{193}}{-8}$$

So, the solutions to the equation are:

$$n = \frac{-3 + \sqrt{193}}{-8} \text{ and } n = \frac{-3 - \sqrt{193}}{-8}$$

or

$$(n = -1.362, \text{ and } n = 2.112)$$

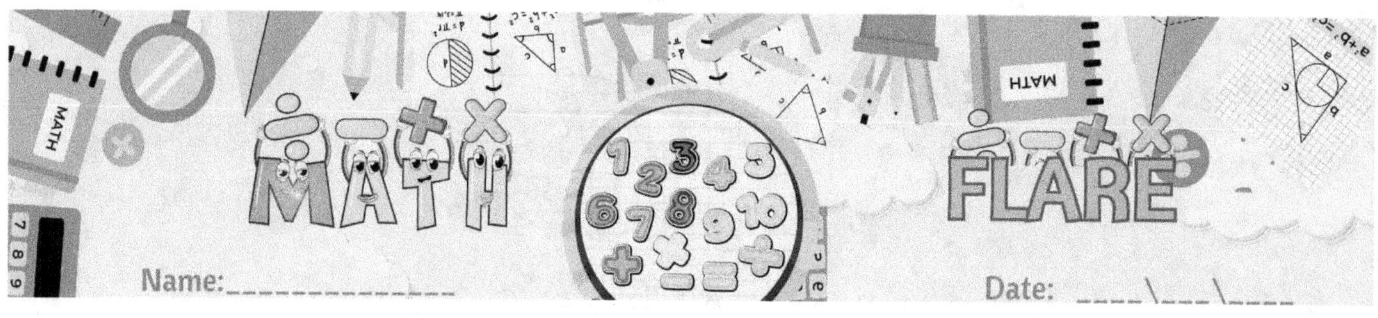

Equations (One Side)
Solve for the variable.

1. $m - 4 = 2$

2. $z \div 5 = 2$

3. $10k - 7 = 53$

4. $4 \times y = 20$

5. $k + 10 = 14$

6. $16 - 8m = 0$

7. $3k - 6 = 0$

8. $4 \times z = 24$

9. $6x + 6 = 54$

10. $18 - 5y = 8$

11. $2 \times x = 4$

12. $y \times 6 = 54$

13. $z \times 10 = 20$

14. $m + 7 = 17$

15. $7 - x = 2$

16. $y \times 5 = 45$

17. $7z - 5 = 30$

18. $2 \times y = 10$

19. $10m - 1 = 49$

20. $9 \times z = 45$

21. $z \div 3 = 6$

22. $3 + 2y = 17$

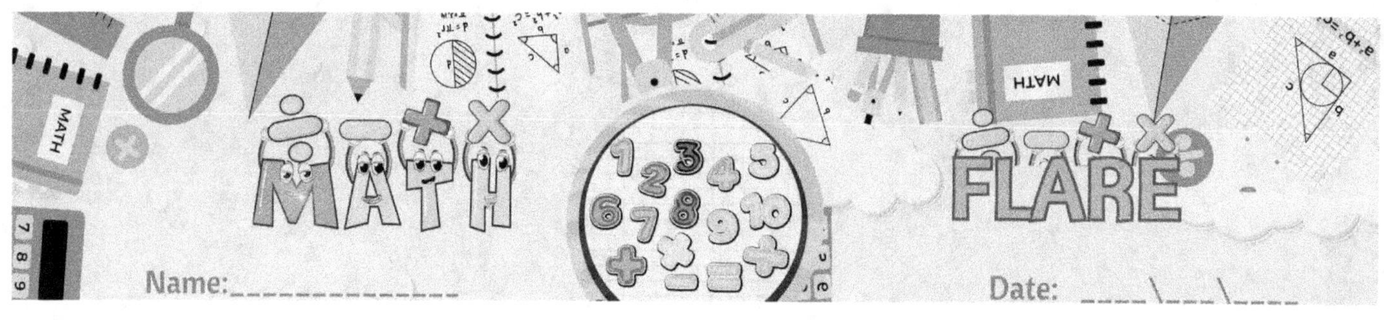

23. $5 \div z = 5$

24. $k \div 9 = 3$

25. $5 \times k = 35$

26. $m \div 1 = 8$

27. $x \div 6 = 3$

28. $9 - m = 8$

29. $z - 3 = 1$

30. $6 - m = 1$

31. $6y + 7 = 55$

32. $z + 4 = 6$

33. $7 + m = 16$

34. $9 + 8y = 25$

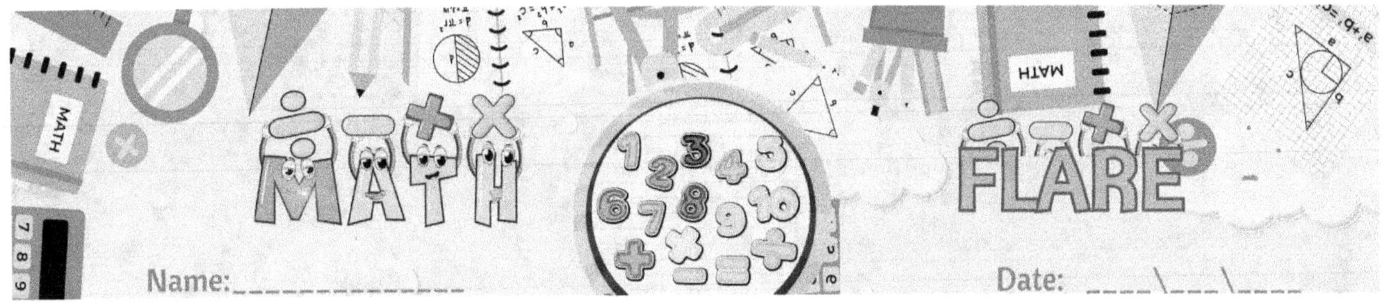

35. $x \times 4 = 12$

36. $2x + 1 = 5$

37. $2 \div m = 2$

38. $k \times 6 = 42$

39. $k \div 4 = 7$

40. $9k + 2 = 83$

41. $y - 1 = 6$

42. $54 \div x = 9$

43. $9 \div k = 1$

44. $28 - 4y = 8$

45. $10 - 1k = 7$

46. $7y - 3 = 32$

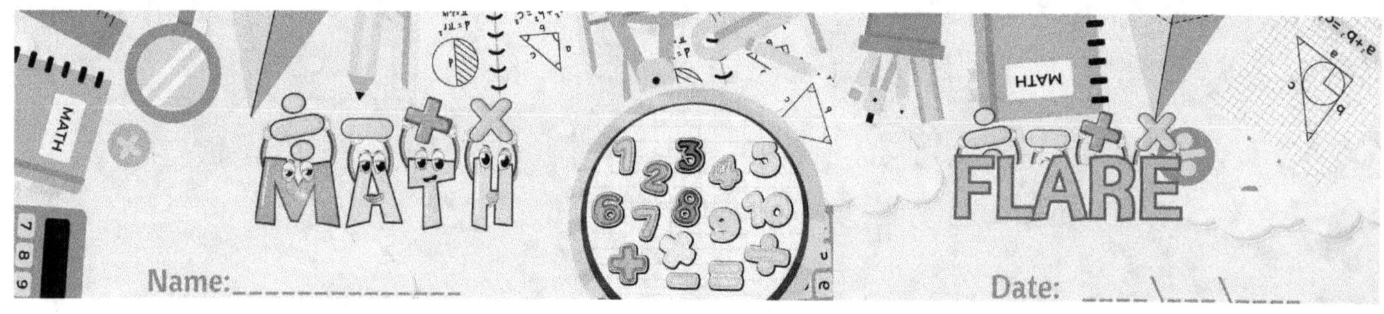

47. $7x - 10 = 39$

48. $1 + 6m = 7$

49. $3x + 9 = 21$

50. $8 - z = 5$

51. $23 - 10x = 3$

52. $x + 3 = 13$

53. $2 + 6z = 50$

54. $y \div 8 = 10$

55. $10m - 4 = 76$

56. $y - 9 = 1$

57. $6 \times k = 60$

58. $z \div 2 = 7$

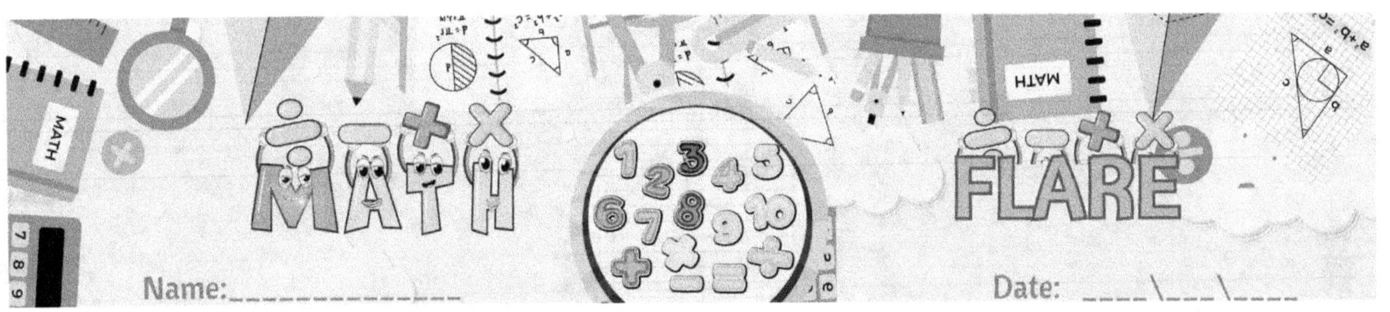

Equations (Two Sides)
Solve for the variable.

59. $2y + 8 = 29 - y$

60. $24 - m = 7m$

61. $2 + k = 2k$

62. $23 - m = 2 + 6m$

63. $2y + 1 = 7 - y$

64. $4k = 20 - k$

65. $5k = 32 + k$

66. $23 + y = 5y + 3$

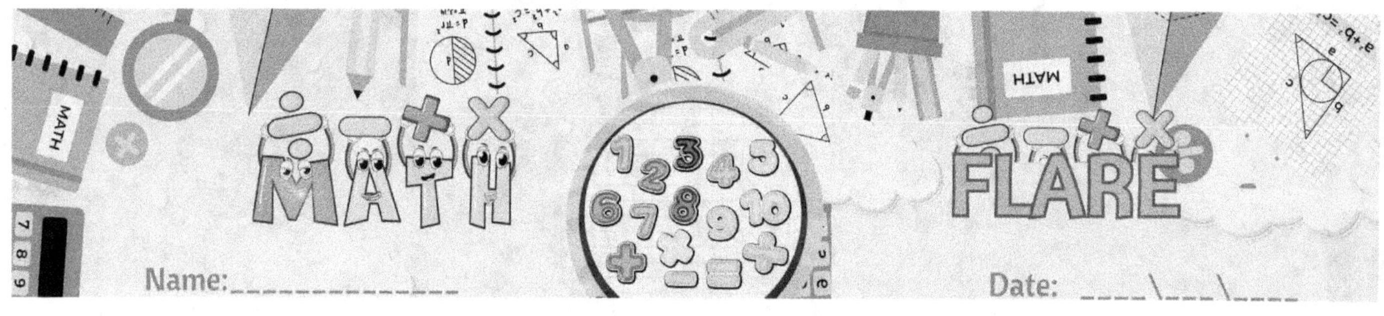

67. $6 + 2k = 9 - k$

68. $69 - z = 5 + 7z$

69. $9 + 8k = 63 - k$

70. $13 + x = 2x + 9$

71. $6x + 7 = 52 + x$

72. $31 + y = 4 + 4y$

73. $42 - x = 6x$

74. $3m = 10 + m$

75. $43 + x = 8x + 8$

76. $4 + 2k = 16 - k$

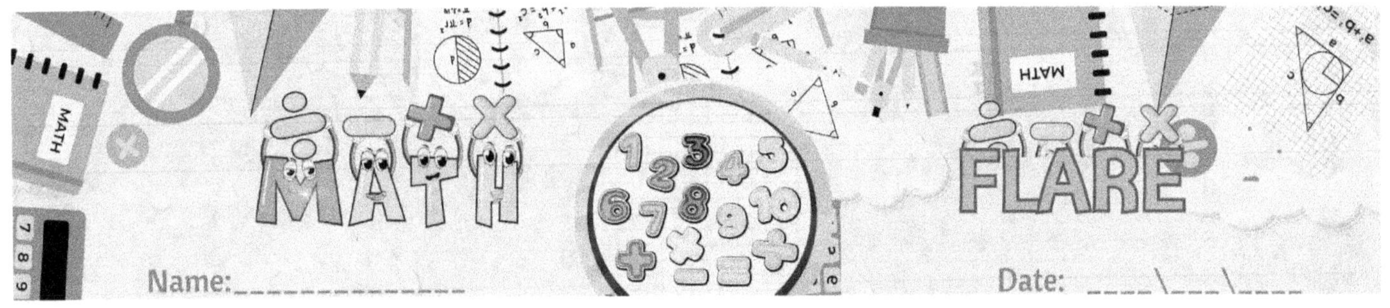

77. $18 - m = 5m$

78. $3 + y = 2y$

79. $32 - m = 3m$

80. $21 - x = 2x$

81. $18 - k = 2k$

82. $4z = 18 + z$

83. $2x = 15 - x$

84. $7y = 42 + y$

85. $4k + 5 = 17 + k$

86. $1 + 2x = 16 - x$

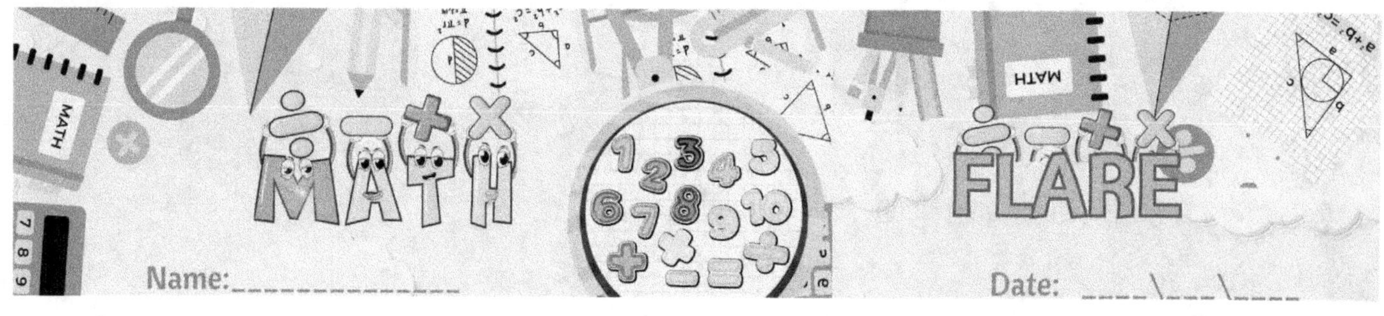

87. $2y = 9 - y$

88. $30 + x = 6 + 7x$

89. $5 + k = 1 + 2k$

90. $6 - z = 2z$

91. $2y + 3 = 6 - y$

92. $57 - z = 1 + 7z$

93. $5k + 9 = 17 + k$

94. $5 + 7y = 29 - y$

95. $30 - z = 4z + 5$

96. $47 - x = 7 + 7x$

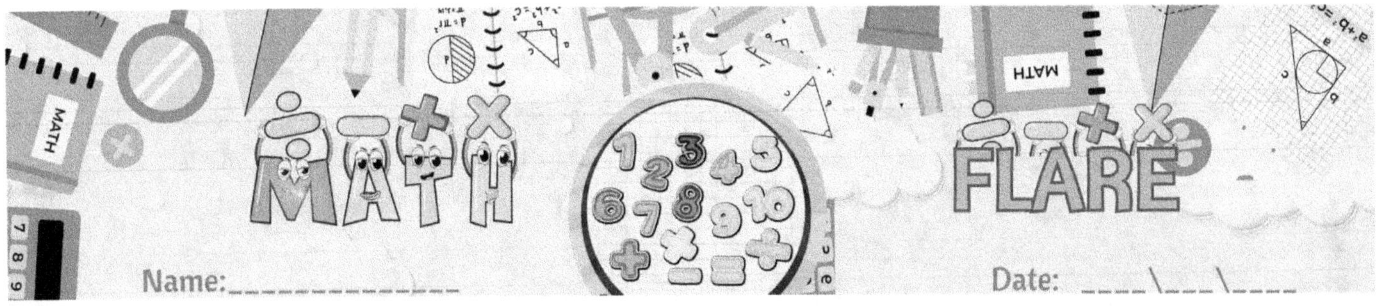

97. $15 + x = 3 + 4x$

98. $42 + y = 7y$

99. $12 - k = 2k + 3$

100. $3m = 12 + m$

101. $3k = 16 + k$

102. $4y = 24 + y$

103. $8m = 81 - m$

104. $6z + 4 = 60 - z$

105. $4k = 40 - k$

106. $4m = 27 + m$

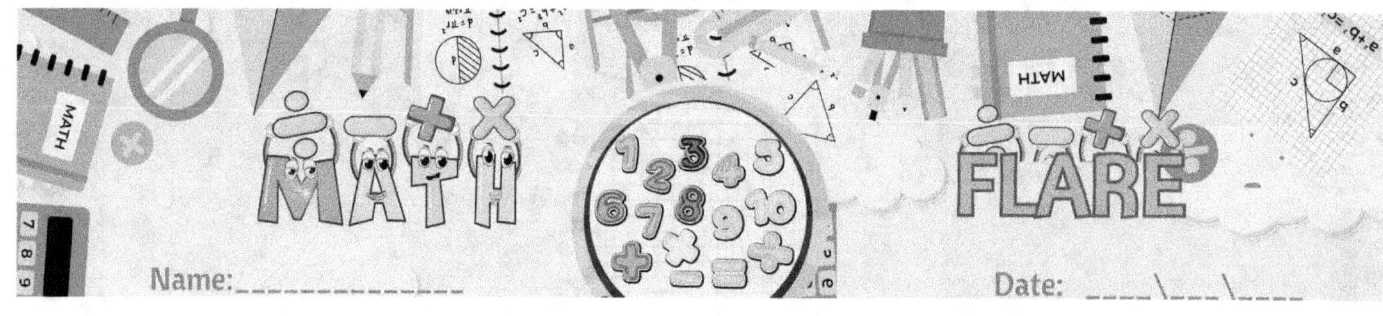

107. $24 + x = 5x$

108. $62 - x = 6x + 6$

109. $5m + 2 = 14 - m$

110. $4z = 18 + z$

111. $2z = 2 + z$

112. $7 + 8x = 70 - x$

113. $42 - x = 6x$

114. $5k = 54 - k$

115. $3k = 4 + k$

116. $4m + 2 = 7 - m$

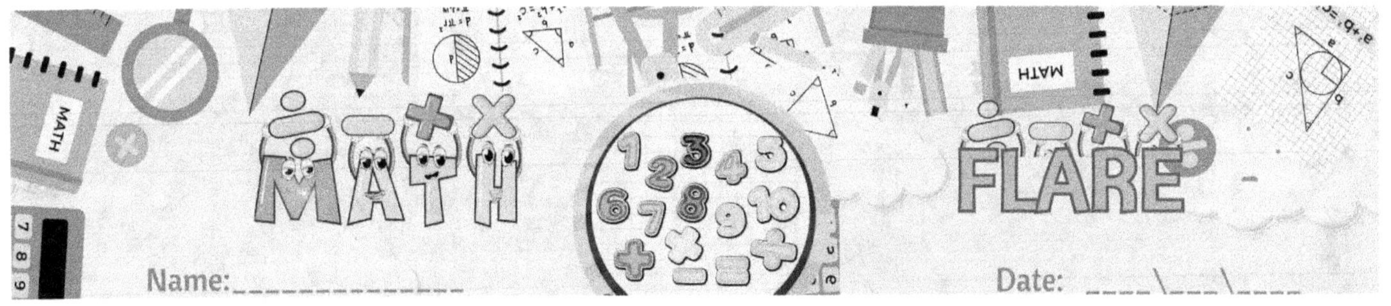

117. $6z = 10 + z$

118. $5k = 28 + k$

119. $29 + z = 5z + 9$

120. $2y = 18 - y$

121. $40 - k = 8 + 3k$

122. $2 + 2y = 6 + y$

123. $27 - y = 2y$

124. $3m + 1 = 37 - m$

125. $7 + y = 8y$

126. $2x = 5 + x$

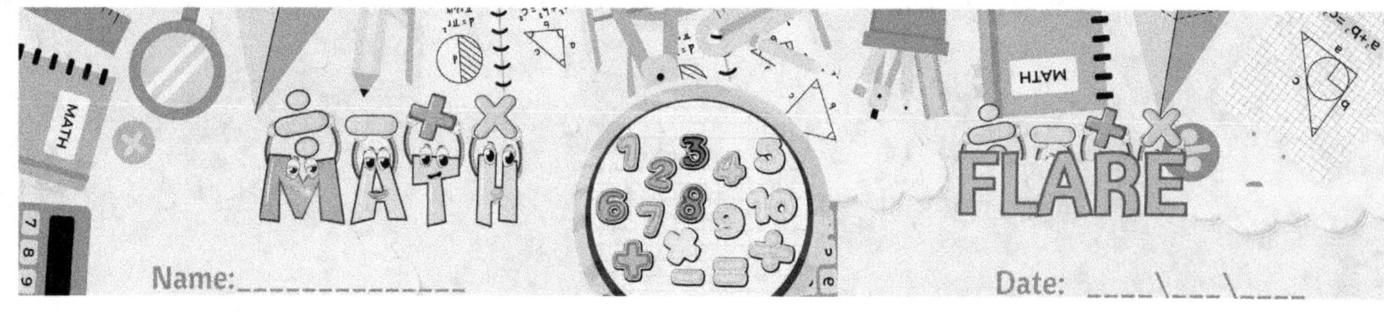

127. $4 + 5y = 8 + y$

128. $7 - z = 6z$

129. $16 - m = 9 + 6m$

130. $6 + 3k = 34 - k$

131. $12 + x = 7x$

132. $10 - x = 7 + 2x$

133. $9 + x = 2x$

134. $45 - k = 4k$

135. $25 + x = 4x + 4$

136. $17 - x = 8 + 2x$

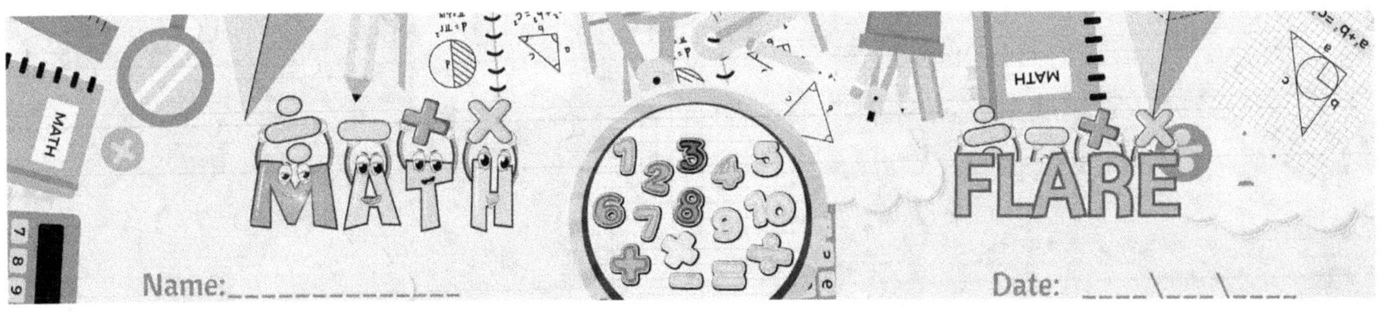

Evaluating Equations

Evaluate each expression when: $x = 4$

137. $9x + 7x - 7 =$

138. $x + 6 + 5x =$

139. $8x - x =$

140. $6x - x =$

141. $2(4 - x) =$

142. $10x + 1 =$

143. $2 + 6x =$

144. $6x + 7 =$

145. $3(4 + x) =$

146. $4x - x =$

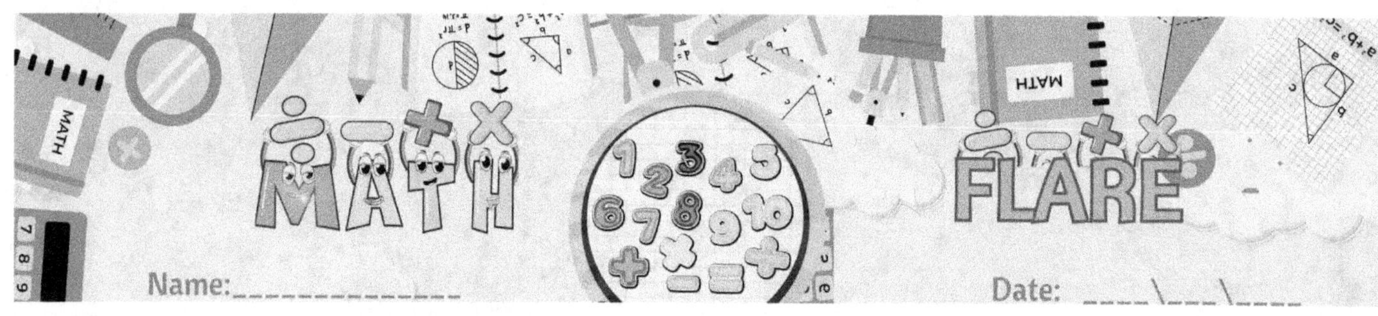

Evaluating Equations

Evaluate each expression when: $x = 6$

147. $8x + 3 =$

148. $9 + x =$

149. $x + 2 + 4x =$

150. $8x - x =$

151. $8x + 8 =$

152. $4 + x =$

153. $x - 2 =$

154. $5x + x =$

155. $4x - x =$

156. $3(6 + x) =$

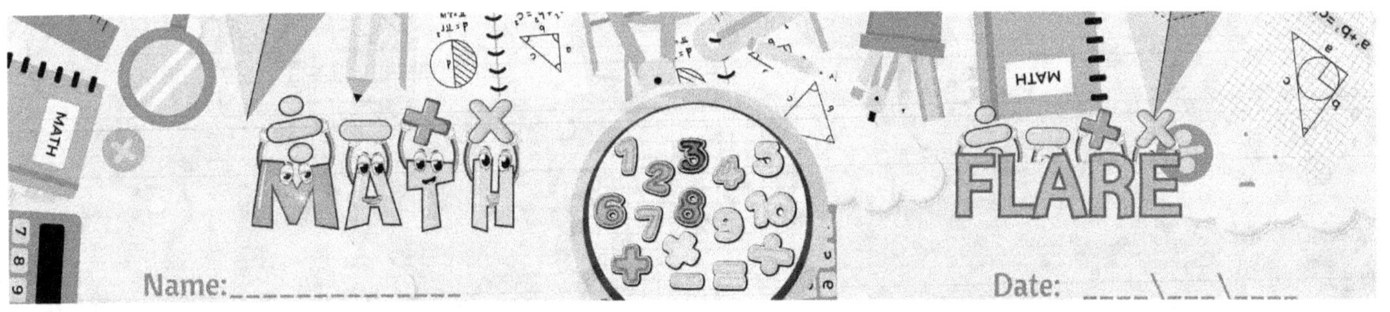

Evaluating Equations

Evaluate each expression when: x = 2

157. $7(8 + x) =$

158. $3 - x =$

159. $2x + 5 =$

160. $6x - 3 =$

161. $x - 2 =$

162. $7 - x =$

163. $x + 6 =$

164. $1(7 + x) =$

165. $1 - x =$

166. $x + 8 =$

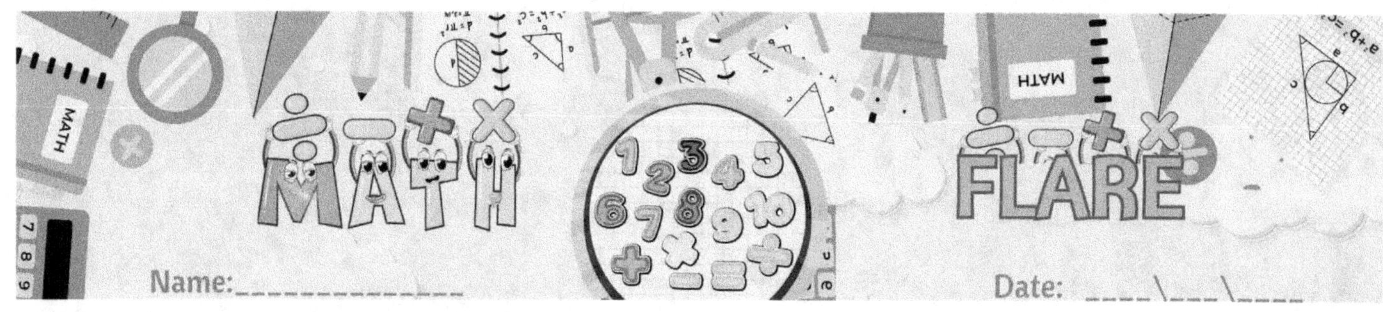

Evaluating Equations

Evaluate each expression when: x = 3

167. $5 - x =$

168. $x - 1 =$

169. $8x + 5 =$

170. $x - 7 =$

171. $6x + x =$

172. $3x + 6 =$

173. $5x + 5 =$

174. $5x + 6 =$

175. $3x + 4 =$

176. $2(10 - x) =$

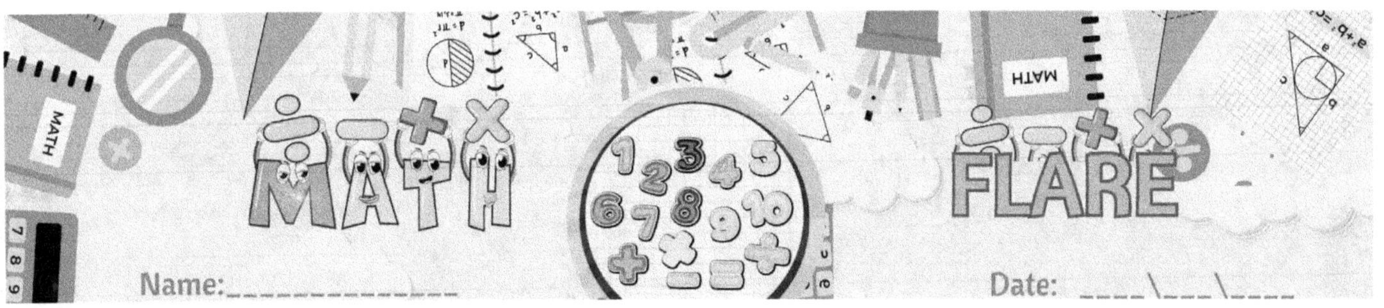

Evaluating Equations

Evaluate each expression when: $x = 5$

177. $x - 8 =$

178. $10 + x =$

179. $5 - x =$

180. $8(8 - x) =$

181. $x + 9 =$

182. $10 + 4x =$

183. $2x + 5 =$

184. $4x + x =$

185. $1 + 4x =$

186. $5x + 3 =$

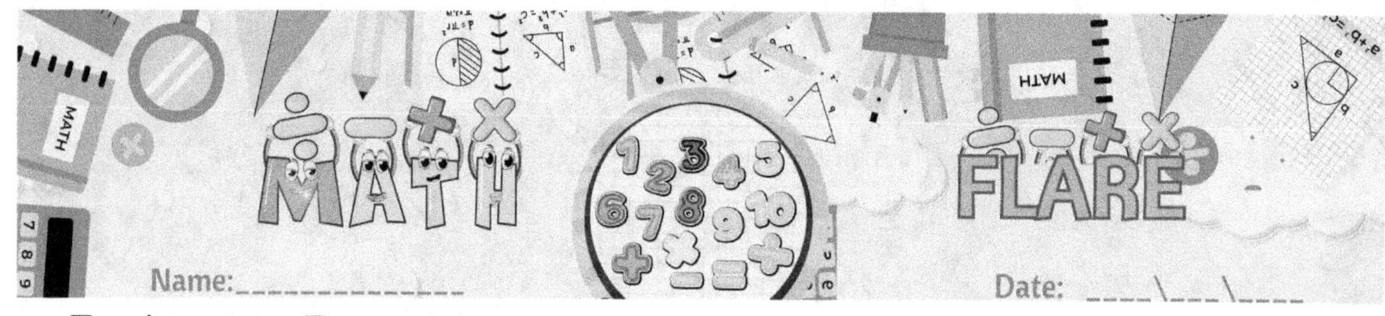

Evaluating Equations

Evaluate each expression when: $x = 5$

187. $x + 6 =$

188. $10x - x =$

189. $10 + x =$

190. $6x + 7 =$

191. $x - 9 =$

192. $6(6 - x) =$

193. $x + 7 =$

194. $8(6 - x) =$

195. $5 + x =$

196. $5x + x =$

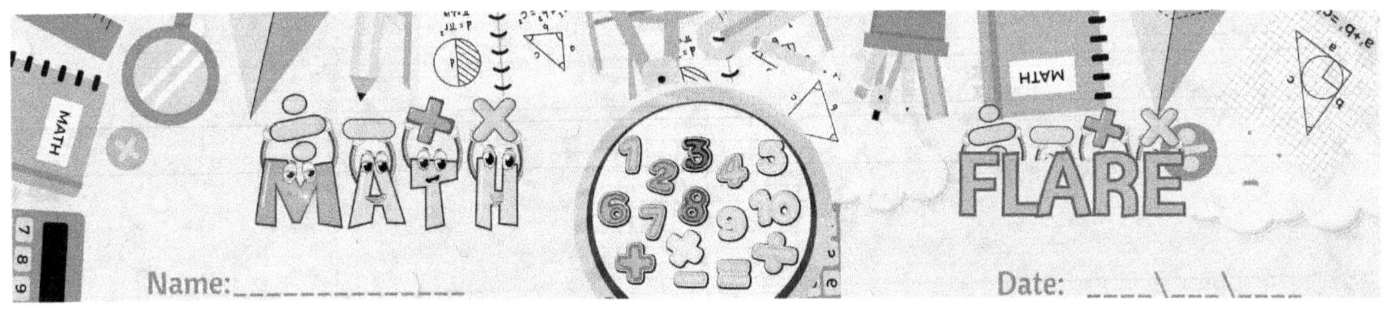

Solving Inequalities

197.

$$3 < 5x$$

198.

$$\frac{y}{-7} \geq 8$$

199.

$$1 + z < 8$$

200.

$$1 < x - {-6}$$

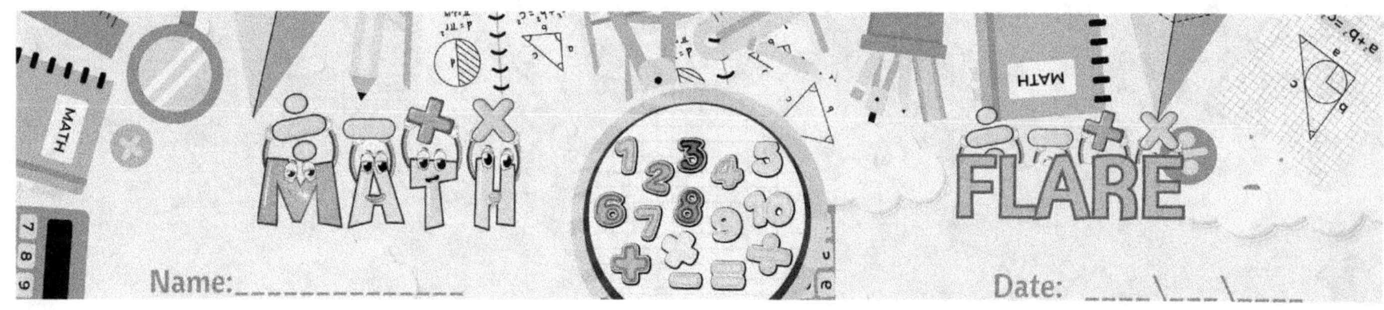

201.

$$-5 + m \le 6$$

202.

$$6 - y \ge 7$$

203.

$$\frac{k}{1} \ge -2$$

204.

$$-9 \le 21\,y$$

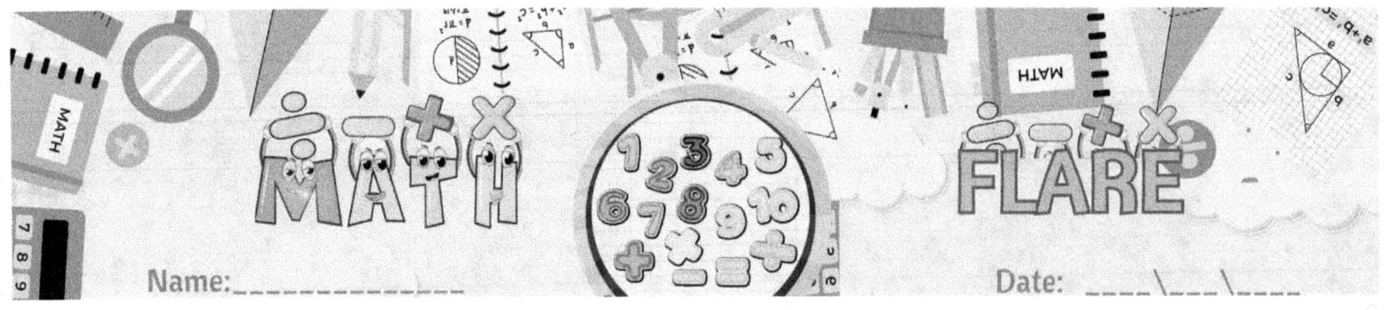

205.
$$k + -1 < 9$$

206.
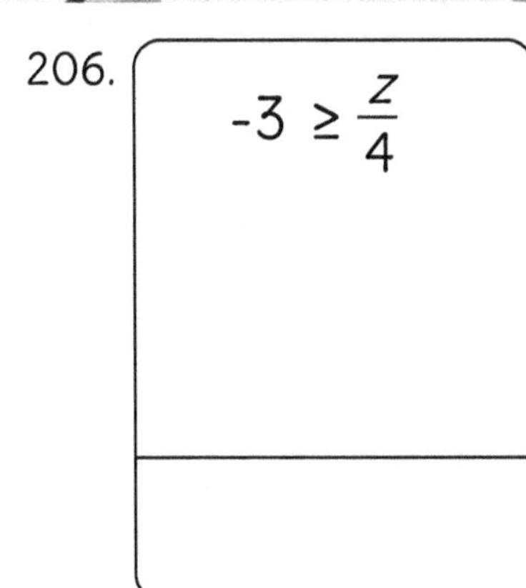
$$-3 \geq \frac{z}{4}$$

207.
$$-8 \geq 14\,m$$

208.
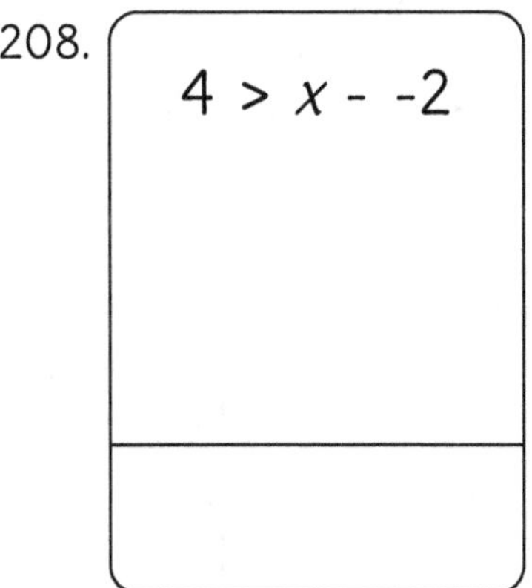
$$4 > x - -2$$

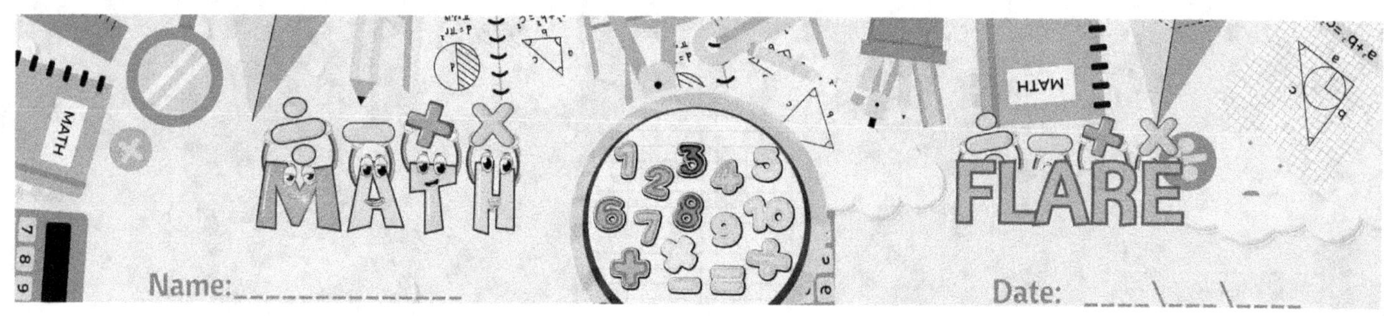

209.

$$2 - k < 9$$

210.

$$-15 \leq -6k$$

211.

$$1 \leq \frac{z}{8}$$

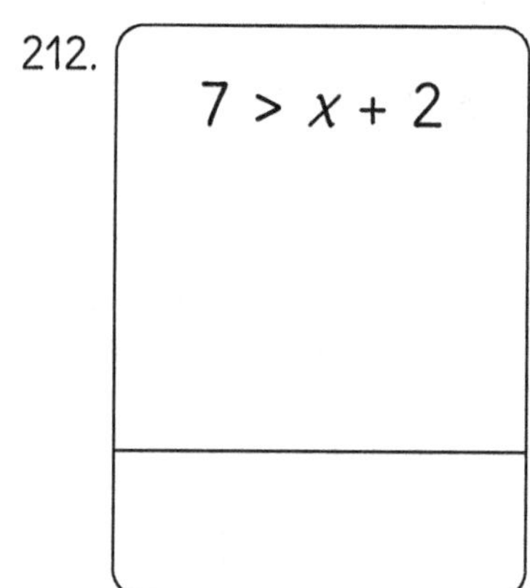

212.

$$7 > x + 2$$

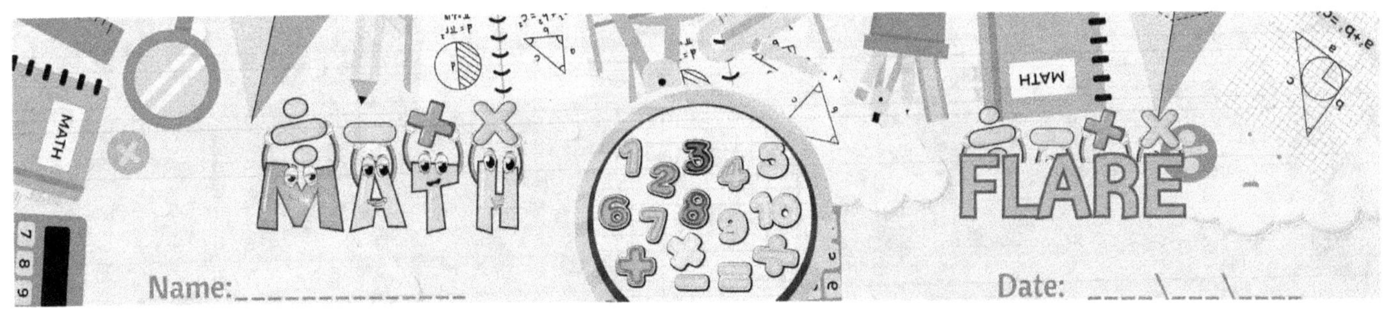

213. $x + 6 > 6$

214. $\dfrac{x}{7} \leq -9$

215. $2k \leq 8$

216. $-6 - z \geq 7$

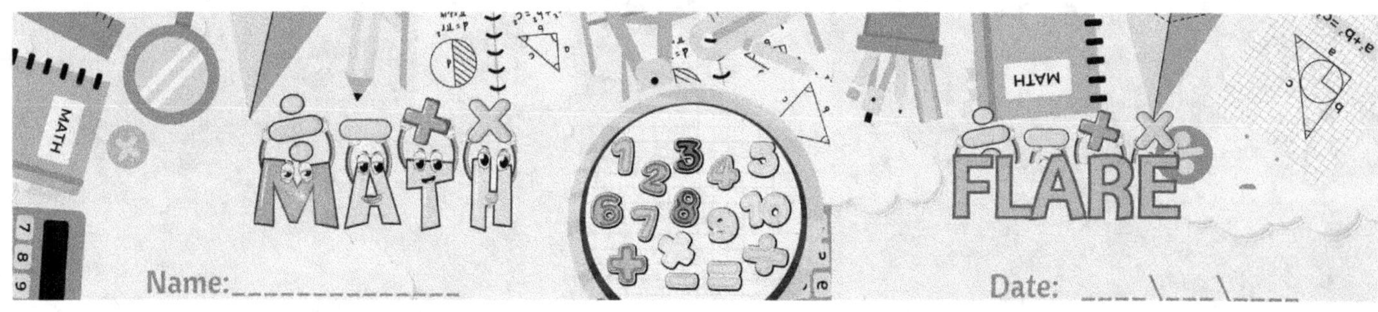

217.

$-12\,z > -15$

218.

$z - 2 > 8$

219.

$-7 < \dfrac{z}{-8}$

220.

$k + -4 < -1$

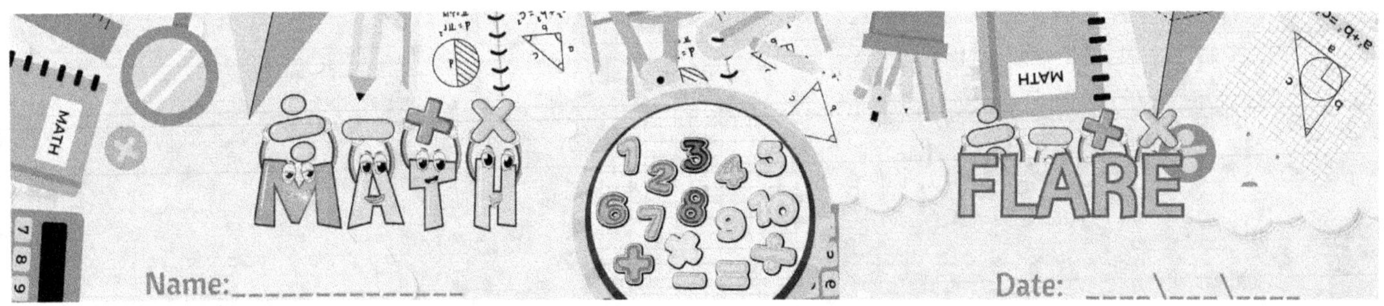

221.

$$10x \leq 12$$

222.

$$-6 + m \geq -1$$

223.

$$m - 3 \leq 5$$

224.

$$\frac{m}{-5} < -2$$

Name:_______________ Date: ____________

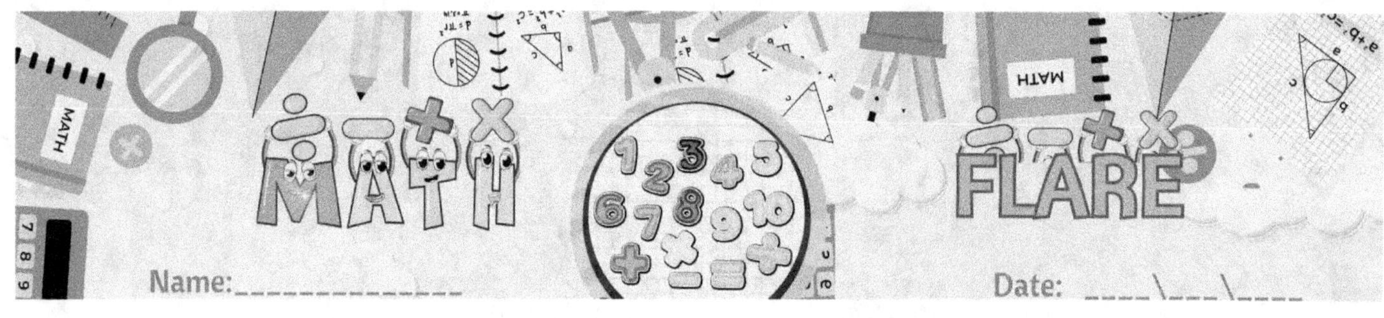

225. $7 \geq 2 + x$

226. $k - -2 > 5$

227. $\frac{z}{-2} \leq 6$

228. $-5 \leq -2x$

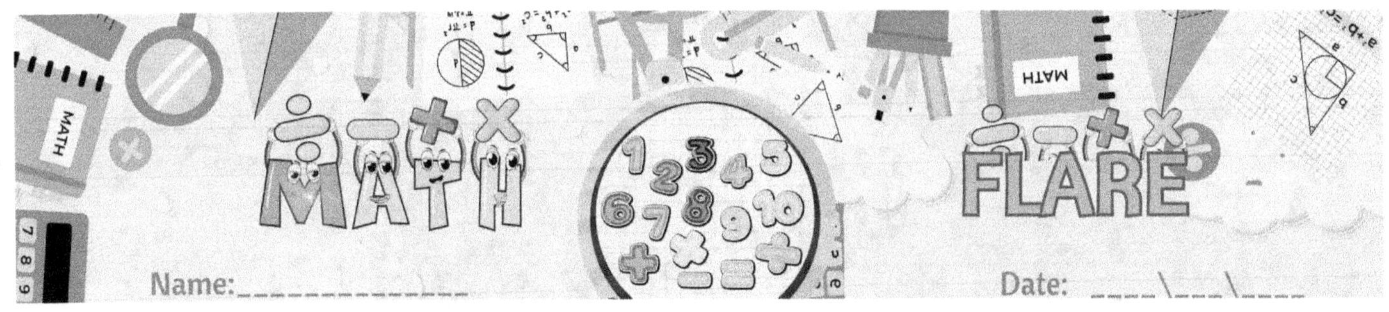

Name: _______________ Date: _______________

229.
$$-6 \geq z + -5$$

230.
$$6\,m < -12$$

231.
$$5 \leq \dfrac{z}{-9}$$

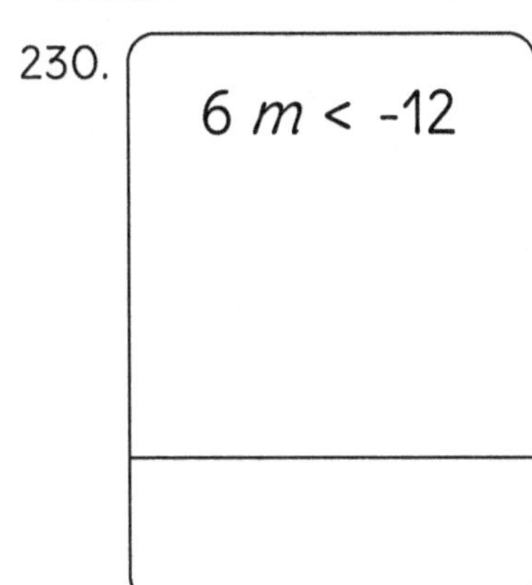

232.
$$8 - y > 9$$

233.

$$6 \geq -4 + k$$

234.

$$9 \leq m - 7$$

235.

$$1 < \frac{k}{4}$$

236.

$$-3z \geq -4$$

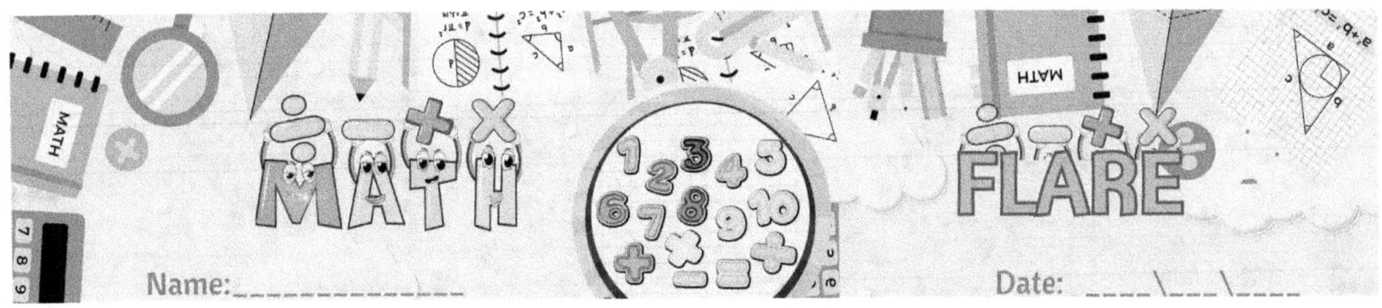

237.

$x + 6 > 9$

238.

$5 < -3\,k$

239.

$8 - y \geq 9$

240.

$\dfrac{k}{5} < 1$

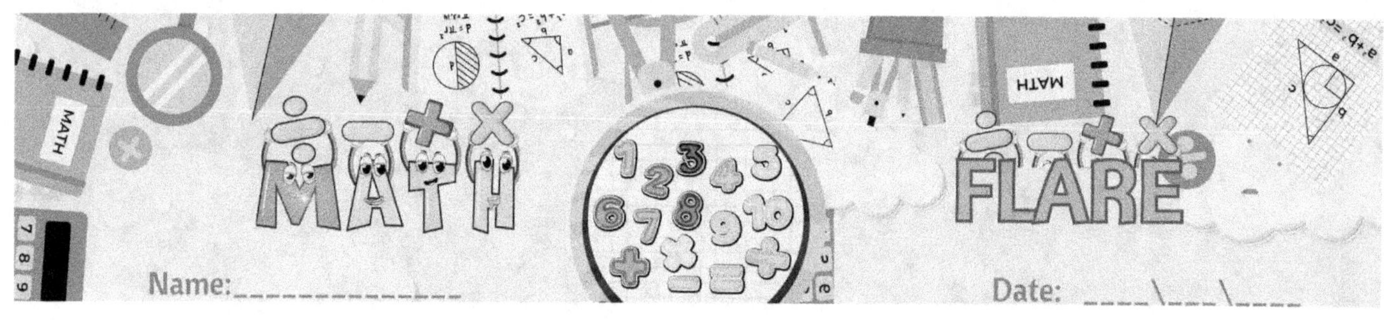

241.

$$-5 \geq -6 + k$$

242.

$$-8 \geq \frac{k}{-5}$$

243.

$$7 \leq y - -4$$

244.

$$-6\,z \geq -4$$

245.

$$6 \geq 2x$$

246.

$$\frac{m}{-8} < 4$$

247.

$$7 \geq y + -8$$

248.

$$-1 - x \leq 3$$

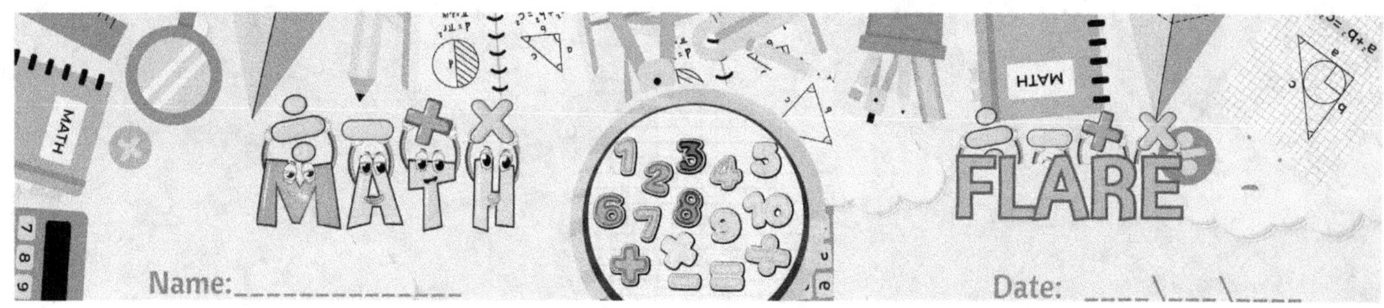

249.
$$1 \geq 2 + m$$

250.
$$20k \leq -12$$

251.
$$4 > \frac{x}{-2}$$

252.
$$4 \leq -2 - y$$

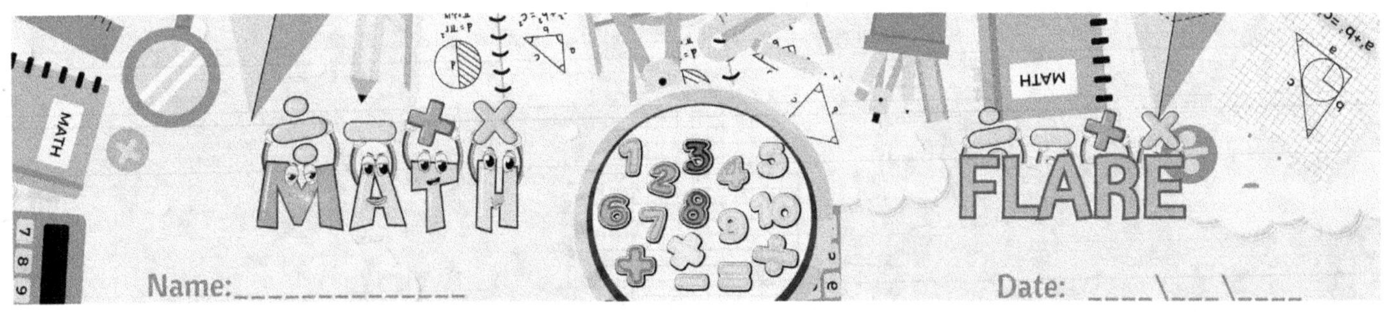

Name: ___________________   Date: _______________

253. $7 > 4 - y$

254.  $-5 < \dfrac{y}{-7}$

255. $-20 \leq 4z$

256. $-2 \geq k + 9$

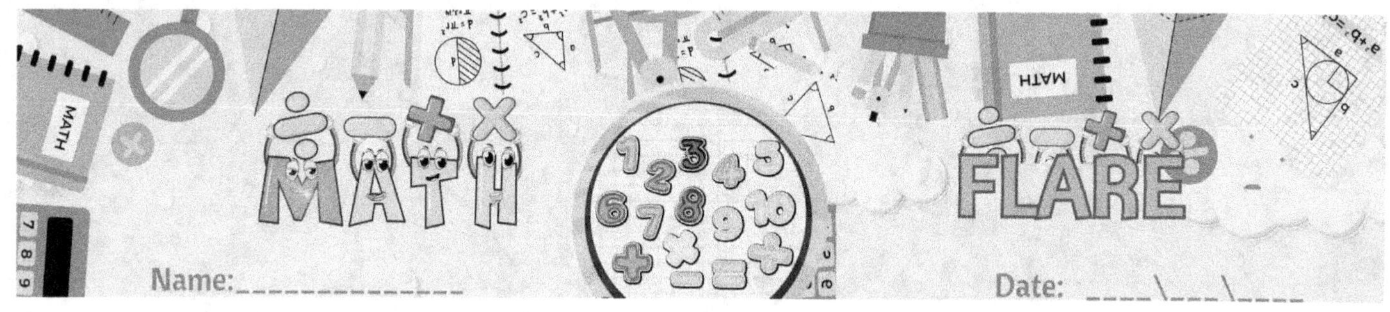

Verbal Algebra

257.   The quotient of a number and ten is 5. Find the number.

258.   Twice a number is 4. What is the number?

259.   Two more than a number is 9. What is the number?

260.   Ten times a number is 0. What is the number?

261.   Eight less than a number is 2. Find the number.

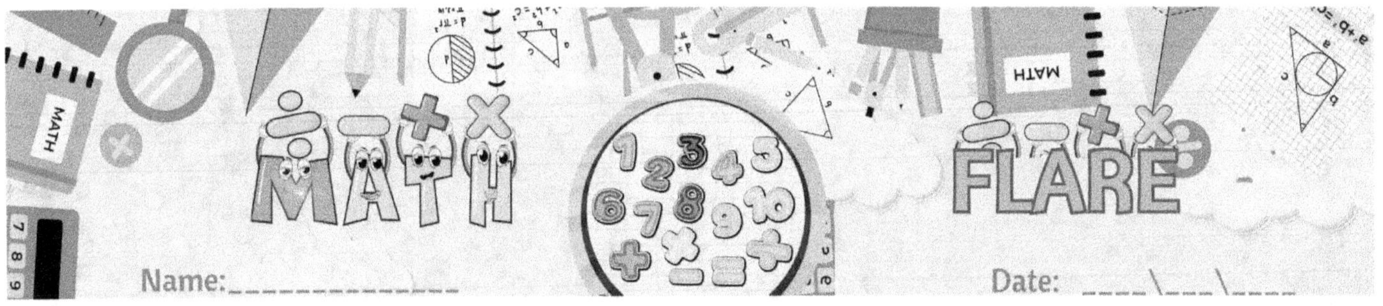

Name:_______________   Date: ____________

262. One-fourth of a number is 1. Find the number.

263. The sum of four consecutive numbers is 18. What are the numbers?

264. The sum of three consecutive numbers is 27. What are the numbers?

265. The sum of three consecutive numbers is 21. What are the numbers?

266. Four more than a number is 7. What is the number?

267.   A number decreased by 9 is 2. Find the number.

268.   One number is two times another. Their sum is 3. Find the numbers.

269.   A number diminished by 3 is 2. Find the number.

270.   The quotient of a number and ten is 8. Find the number.

271.   The sum of a number and eight is 17. Find the number.

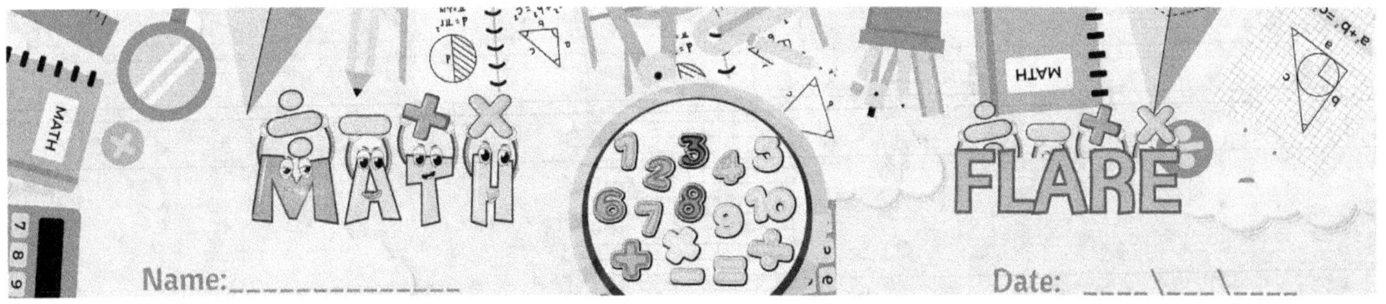

272. The sum of two consecutive numbers is 13. What are the numbers?

273. When a number is divided by four, the result is 9. What is the number?

274. The quotient of a number and two is 9. Find the number.

275. The product of two and a number is 6. What is the number?

276. A number increased by two is 8. Find the number.

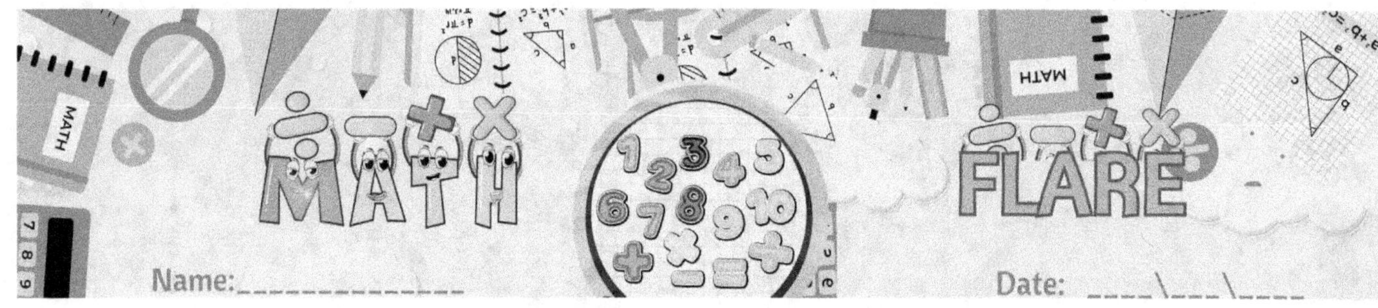

277. The quotient of a number and five is 2. Find the number.

278. Five more than a number is 7. What is the number?

279. A number diminished by 8 is 9. Find the number.

280. The sum of a number and nine is 15. Find the number.

281. The sum of three consecutive numbers is 6. What are the numbers?

282.   One number is four times another. Their sum is 5. Find the numbers.

283.   The product of two and a number is 18. What is the number?

284.   Two-fourths of a number is 4. Find the number.

285.   A number diminished by 5 is 2. Find the number.

286.   Three less than a number is 8. Find the number.

287.   Eight more than a number is 17. What is the number?

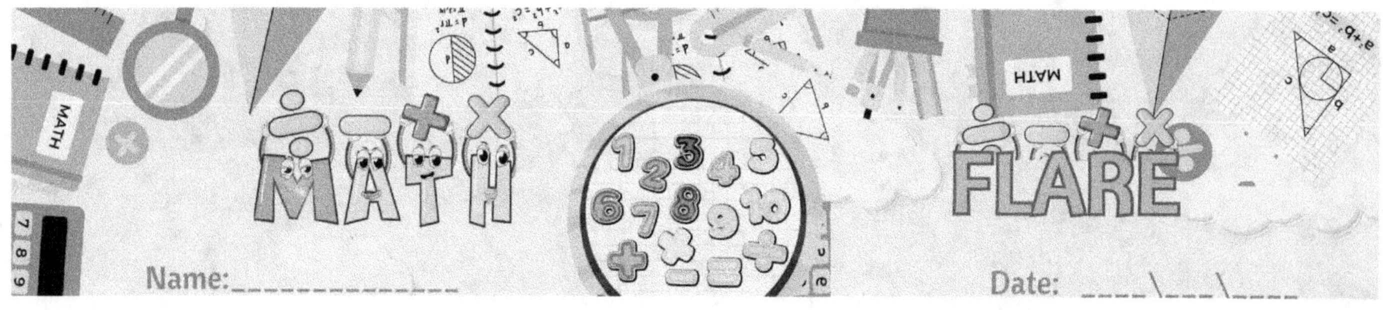

288. The sum of a number and four is 7. Find the number.

289. A number diminished by 1 is 9. Find the number.

290. The sum of two consecutive numbers is 9. What are the numbers?

291. The product of three and a number is 3. What is the number?

292. The quotient of a number and four is 9. Find the number.

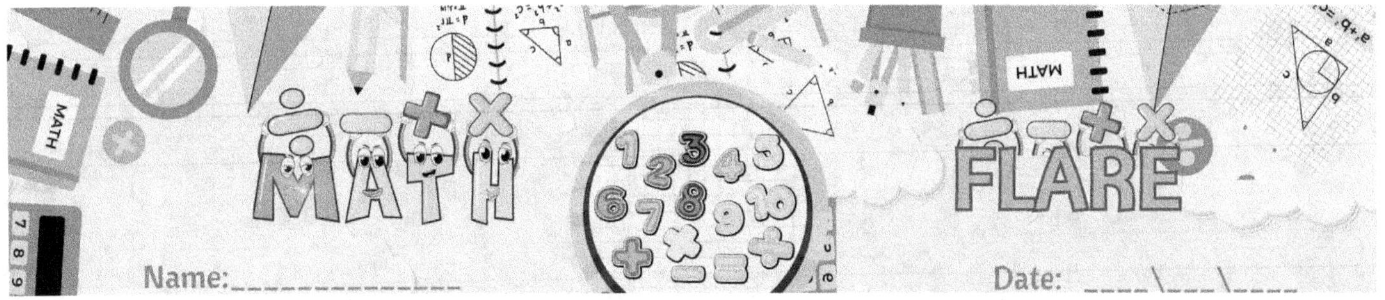

293. One less than five times a number is 59. Find the number.

294. The sum of four consecutive numbers is 10. What are the numbers?

295. One less than a number is 2. Find the number.

296. One number is nine times another. Their sum is 40. Find the numbers.

297. One less than twice a number is 15. Find the number.

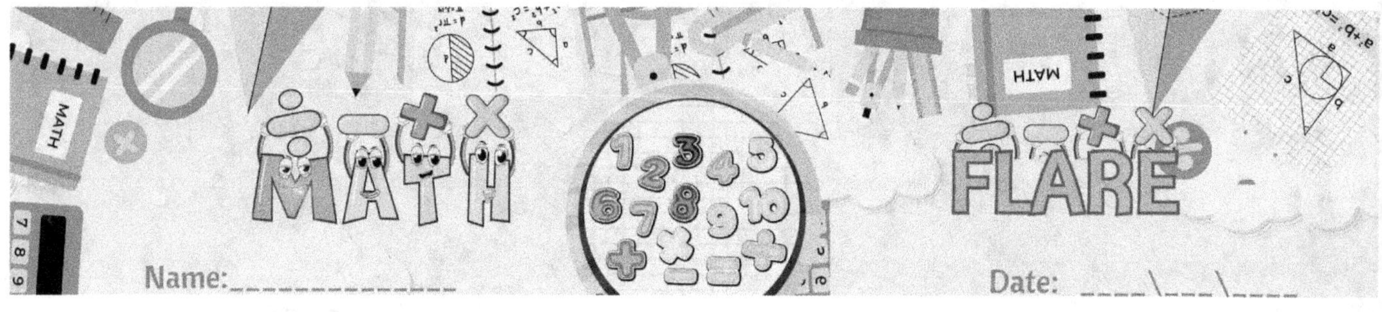

Linear Equations

1. $x + -1 = -10$

2. $-1x + 3 = -1$

3. $7x + -10 = -24$

4. $-5x + 9 = 44$

5. $-10x + 9 = -41$

6. $-8x + -3 = 13$

7. $-8x + -3 = 61$

8. $5x + -8 = -48$

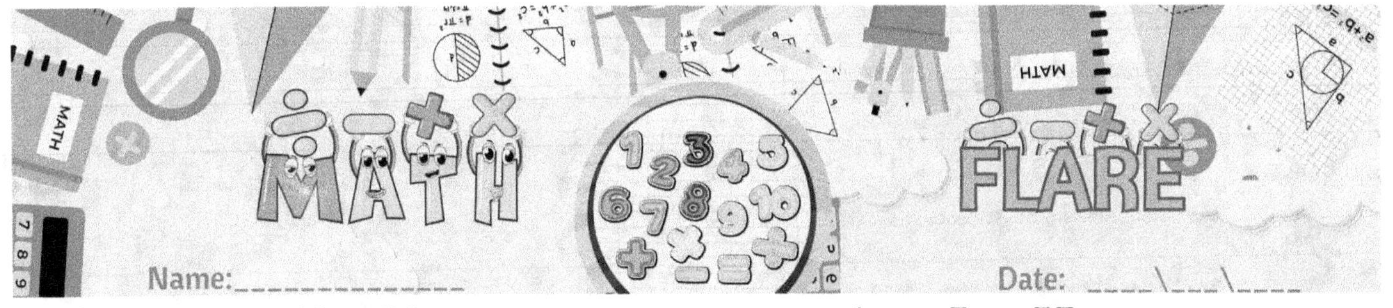

9. $-8x + -10 = 22$

13. $-4x + -5 = -37$

10. $10x + 7 = 97$

14. $5x + 6 = -19$

11. $5x + -7 = -32$

15. $-3x + 8 = -19$

12. $8x + -7 = -39$

16. $6x + 6 = 12$

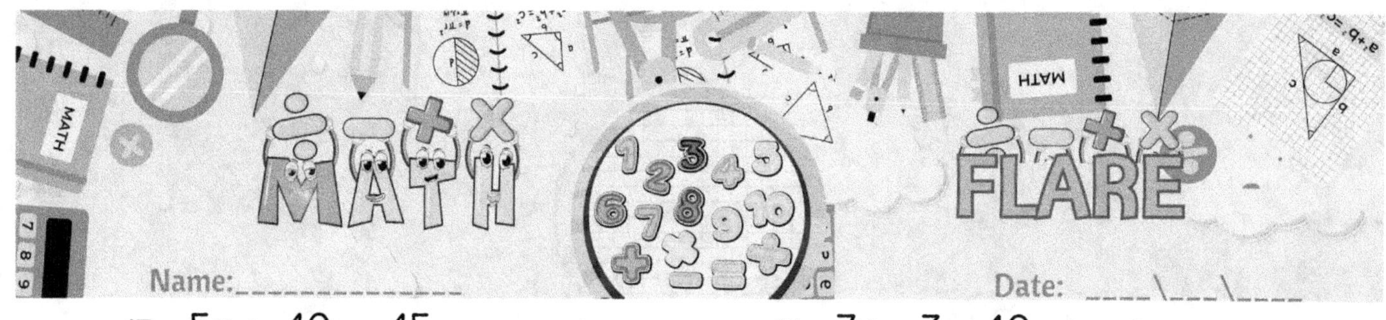

17. $-5x + -10 = -15$

21. $-7x + 3 = 10$

18. $-8x + -1 = -25$

22. $-5x + 1 = 11$

19. $2x + 0 = 4$

23. $-5x + 2 = 2$

20. $8x + 3 = 43$

24. $-8x + -8 = -8$

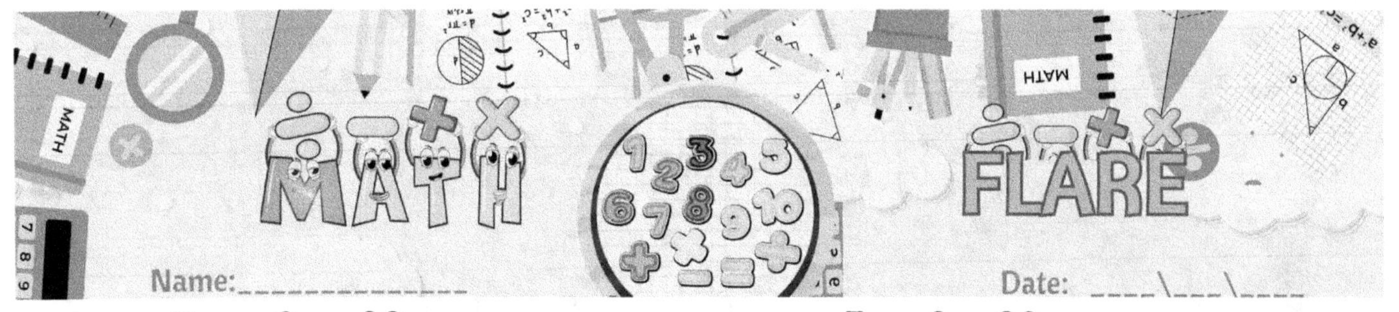

25. $7x + -8 = -29$

29. $-7x + 8 = 22$

26. $-6x + -10 = -22$

30. $2x + -1 = -15$

27. $10x + 4 = 84$

28. $-2x + -7 = -9$

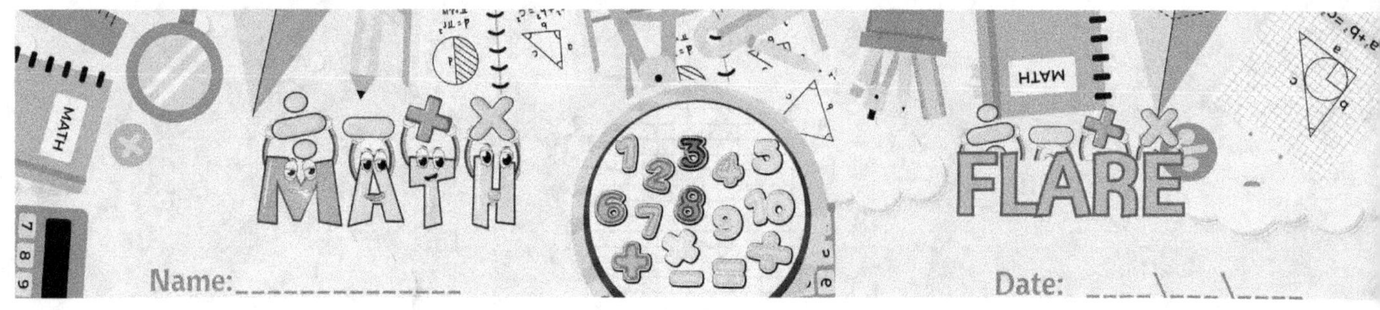

Find Slope from Two Points

1. (-1, 6) and (-5, -6)

5. (1, 4) and (10, 4)

2. (-10, -80) and (-7, -53)

6. (6, -13) and (3, -4)

3. (5, -13) and (10, -23)

7. (-4, -1) and (-3, -1)

4. (10, -65) and (1, -11)

8. (8, 78) and (1, 8)

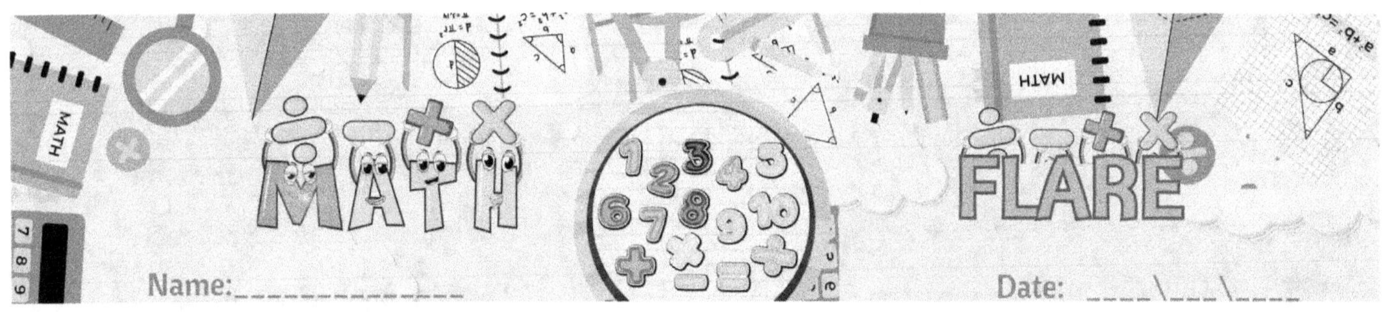

9. (4, 12) and (-2, -6)

13. (5, -22) and (2, -13)

10. (-8, -33) and (0, -1)

14. (8, -27) and (-4, 21)

11. (-3, -34) and (-5, -54)

15. (-1, 13) and (9, -67)

12. (6, -57) and (-7, 47)

16. (10, -5) and (7, -5)

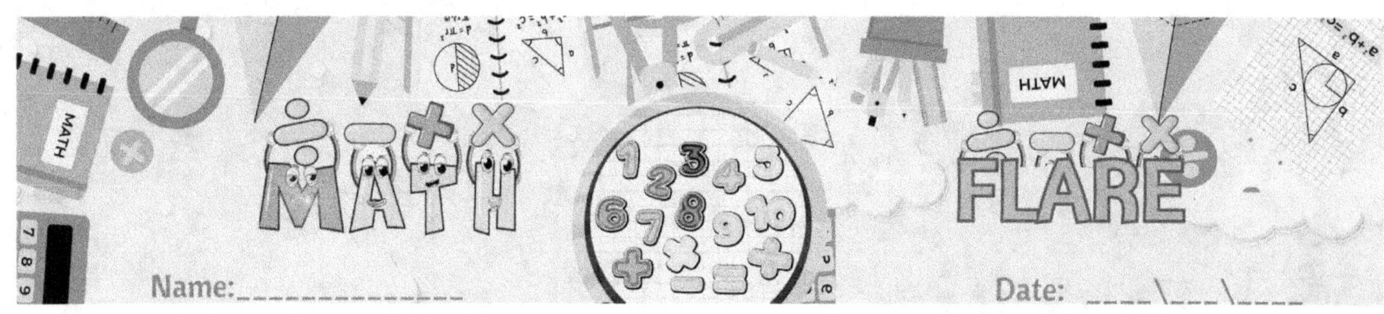

17. (10, -14) and (2, 2)

21. (-8, -10) and (8, 22)

18. (6, 7) and (-7, 7)

22. (-3, 2) and (1, 6)

19. (-5, -17) and (6, 38)

23. (3, -24) and (8, -69)

20. (6, 2) and (-2, -14)

24. (-10, -92) and (0, 8)

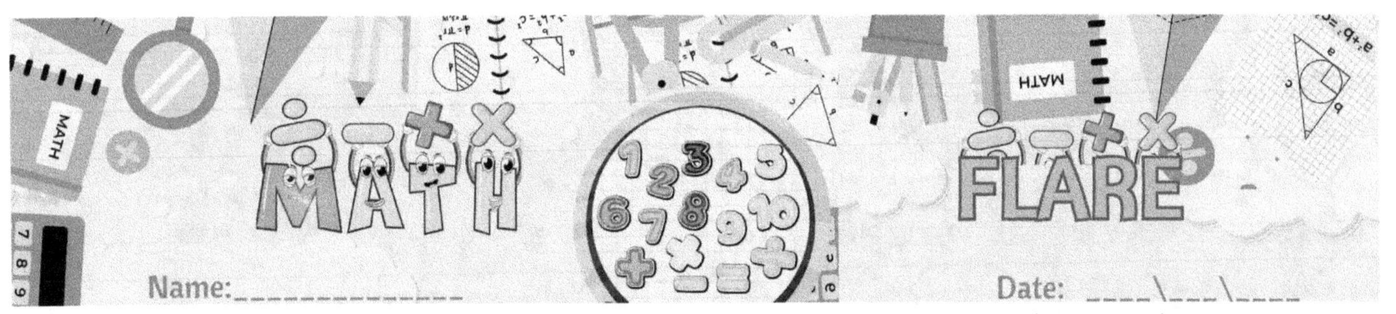

25. (0, 0) and (-6, -54)

29. (7, 48) and (-8, -57)

26. (-1, -8) and (9, 52)

30. (-7, 32) and (3, -18)

27. (-9, 36) and (6, -39)

28. (10, 2) and (-6, 2)

Quadratic Equations

1. $-5x^2 + 4x + 15 = 0$

2. $10x^2 + 5 = 0$

3. $-4k^2 + 2k + 19 = 0$

4. $-5n^2 + 5n + 30 = 0$

5. $-2r^2 + 13 = 0$

6. $-10r^2 + 4r - 4 = 0$

7. $4r^2 - 6r + 3 = 0$

8. $-4v^2 + 12v + 135 = 0$

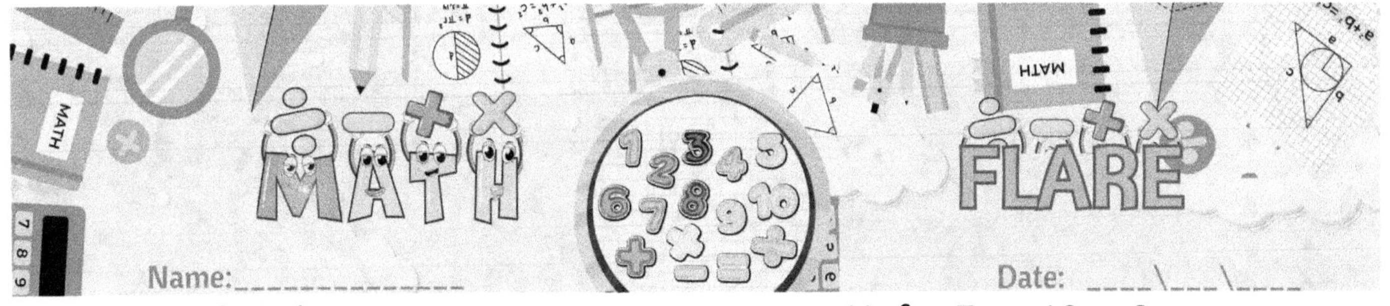

Name:_______________   Date: ____________

9. $4k^2 + 9k + 5 = 0$

13. $-11n^2 + 7n + 10 = 0$

10. $6a^2 - 5a - 14 = 0$

14. $12n^2 + 8n + 10 = 0$

11. $6x^2 - 12 = 0$

15. $6n^2 - 2n - 5 = 0$

12. $8x^2 - 8x - 8 = 0$

16. $5x^2 + 4x - 1 = 0$

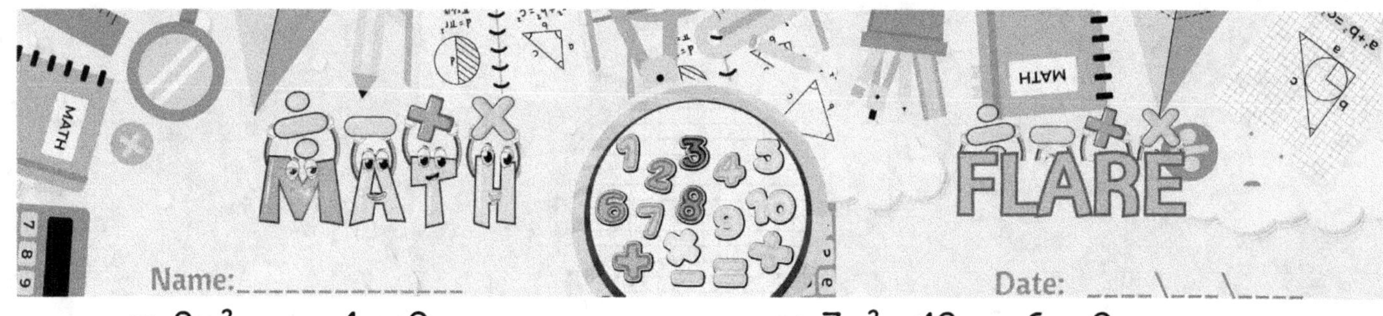

Name:______________________   Date: _______________

17. $8n^2 + n - 4 = 0$

18. $4x^2 + 2x - 90 = 0$

19. $-8n^2 + 12n - 1 = 0$

20. $-2x^2 - 6x - 4 = 0$

21. $7n^2 - 12n - 6 = 9$

22. $10x^2 + 3x + 6 = 2$

23. $12n^2 - 5 = 6$

24. $-3n^2 + 8n + 12 = -4$

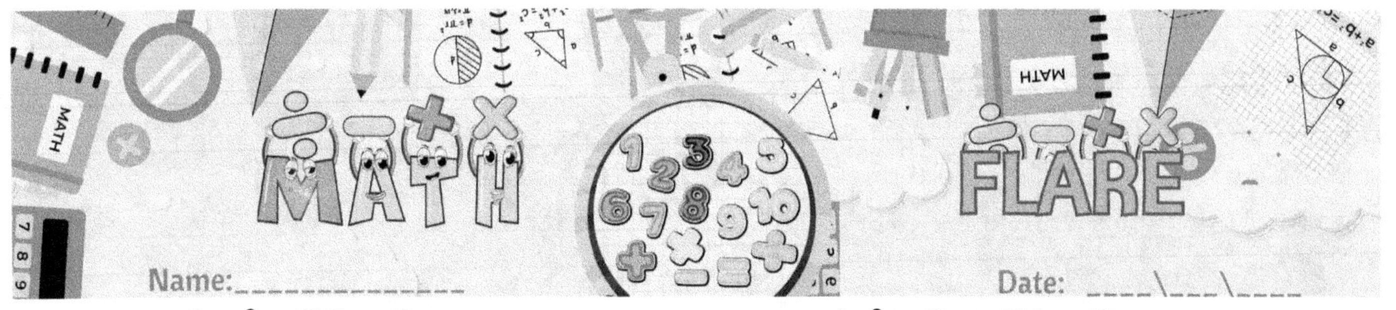

25. $-2p^2 + 59 = 9$

29. $4v^2 - 8v - 74 = 3$

26. $2r^2 + 10r + 4 = -8$

30. $-11x^2 - 7x + 19 = 11$

27. $-10n^2 + 17 = 9$

31. $x^2 + 7x - 5 = -8$

28. $-7n^2 + 5n - 5 = -6$

32. $5k^2 + 7k - 5 = -9$

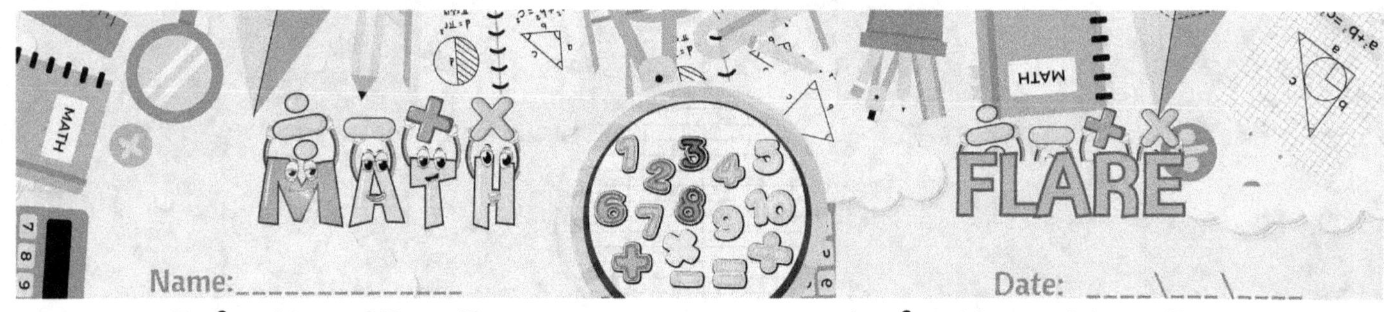

33. $3x^2 - 11x - 27 = -7$

37. $-4m^2 - 11m - 14 = -5$

34. $3n^2 + 12n - 21 = -10$

38. $6n^2 + 7n - 5 = 8$

35. $-v^2 + 6v + 38 = -2$

39. $-4n^2 + n - 1 = 5$

36. $3v^2 - 7v - 36 = -10$

40. $-4n^2 + 5 = -4$

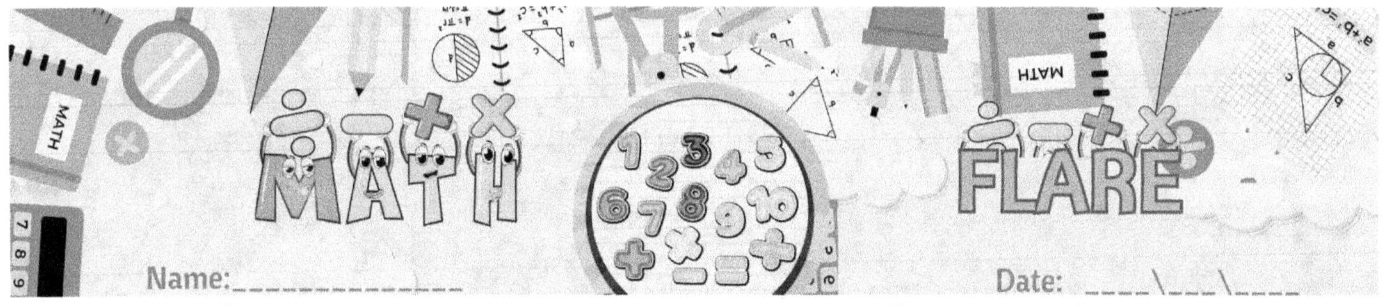

Name:________________   Date: _______________

41. $-m^2 = -24$

45. $-4n^2 - 2n = -4$

42. $m^2 = 10m + 119$

46. $-4x^2 + 36 = 7x$

43. $-6b^2 - 4b = -130$

47. $b^2 + 5b = -6$

44. $-m^2 = -144$

48. $2r^2 - 20 = -12r$

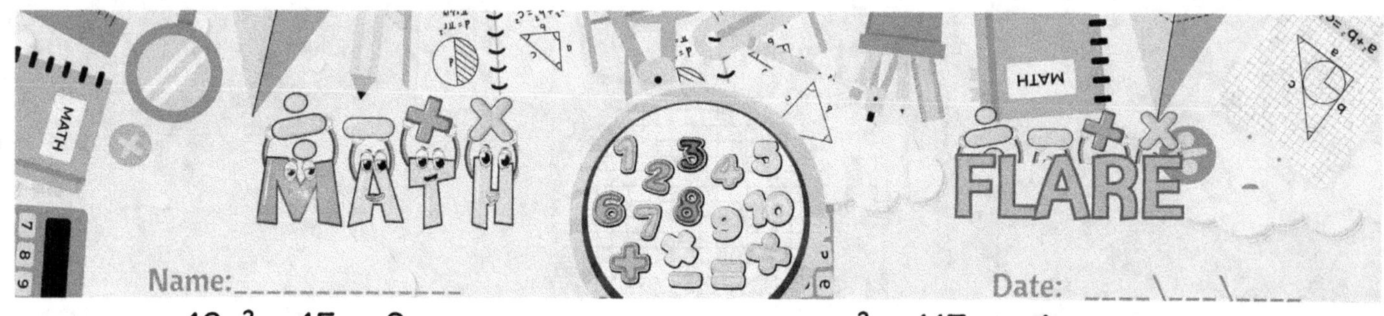

49. $-12r^2 + 15 = 0$

53. $-x^2 + 117 = -4x$

50. $8b^2 = 14 - 7b$

54. $3b^2 = 36 + 12b$

51. $11v^2 + 9v = 1$

55. $11a^2 = 23$

52. $-4x^2 = -144$

56. $-11n^2 = 11n - 15$

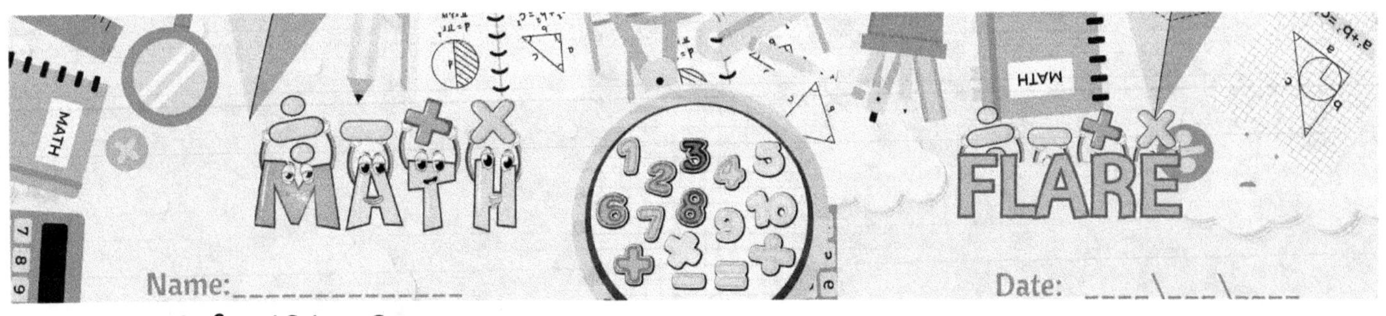

57. $4x^2 - 121 = 0$

58. $8x^2 + x = -4$

59. $6x^2 - 20 = -5x$

60. $m^2 = 5m + 13$

ANSWERS

Page 1: Equations (One Side)

1. m = 6	2. z = 10	3. k = 6	4. y = 5	5. k = 4	6. m = 2
7. k = 2	8. z = 6	9. x = 8	10. y = 2	11. x = 2	12. y = 9
13. z = 2	14. m = 10	15. x = 5	16. y = 9	17. z = 5	18. y = 5
19. m = 5	20. z = 5	21. z = 18	22. y = 7	23. z = 1	24. k = 27
25. k = 7	26. m = 8	27. x = 18	28. m = 1	29. z = 4	30. m = 5
31. y = 8	32. z = 2	33. m = 9	34. y = 2	35. x = 3	36. x = 2
37. m = 1	38. k = 7	39. k = 28	40. k = 9	41. y = 7	42. x = 6
43. k = 9	44. y = 5	45. k = 3	46. y = 5	47. x = 7	48. m = 1
49. x = 4	50. z = 3	51. x = 2	52. x = 10	53. z = 8	54. y = 80
55. m = 8	56. y = 10	57. k = 10	58. z = 14		

Page 6: Equations (Two Sides)

59. y = 7	60. m = 3	61. k = 2	62. m = 3	63. y = 2
64. k = 4	65. k = 8	66. y = 5	67. k = 1	68. z = 8
69. k = 6	70. x = 4	71. x = 9	72. y = 9	73. x = 6
74. m = 5	75. x = 5	76. k = 4	77. m = 3	78. y = 3
79. m = 8	80. x = 7	81. k = 6	82. z = 6	83. x = 5
84. y = 7	85. k = 4	86. x = 5	87. y = 3	88. x = 4
89. k = 4	90. z = 2	91. y = 1	92. z = 7	93. k = 2
94. y = 3	95. z = 5	96. x = 5	97. x = 4	98. y = 7

99. k = 3   100. m = 6   101. k = 8   102. y = 8   103. m = 9

104. z = 8   105. k = 8   106. m = 9   107. x = 6   108. x = 8

109. m = 2   110. z = 6   111. z = 2   112. x = 7   113. x = 6

114. k = 9   115. k = 2   116. m = 1   117. z = 2   118. k = 7

119. z = 5   120. y = 6   121. k = 8   122. y = 4   123. y = 9

124. m = 9   125. y = 1   126. x = 5   127. y = 1   128. z = 1

129. m = 1   130. k = 7   131. x = 2   132. x = 1   133. x = 9

134. k = 9   135. x = 7   136. x = 3

Page 14: Evaluating Equations

137. 57   138. 30   139. 28   140. 20   141. 0   142. 41   143. 26

144. 31   145. 24   146. 12

Page 15: Evaluating Equations

147. 51   148. 15   149. 32   150. 42   151. 56   152. 10   153. 4   154. 36

155. 18   156. 36

Page 16: Evaluating Equations

157. 70   158. 1   159. 9   160. 9   161. 0   162. 5   163. 8   164. 9

165. -1   166. 10

Page 17: Evaluating Equations

167. 2   168. 2   169. 29   170. -4   171. 21   172. 15   173. 20   174. 21

175. 13   176. 14

Page 18: Evaluating Equations

177. -3   178. 15   179. 0   180. 24   181. 14   182. 30   183. 15   184. 25

185. 21   186. 28

Page 19: Evaluating Equations

187. 11   188. 45   189. 15   190. 37   191. -4   192. 6   193. 12   194. 8

195. 10   196. 30

Page 20: Solving Inequalities

197. $x > 3/5$ 198. $y \le -56$ 199. $z < 7$ 200. $x > -5$

201. $m \le 11$ 202. $y \le -1$ 203. $k \ge -2$ 204. $y \ge -3/7$

205. $k < 10$ 206. $z \le -12$ 207. $m \le -4/7$ 208. $x < 2$

209. $k > -7$ 210. $k \le 5/2$ 211. $z \ge 8$ 212. $x < 5$

213. $x > 0$ 214. $x \le -63$ 215. $k \le 4$ 216. $z \le -13$

217. $z < 5/4$ 218. $z > 10$ 219. $z < 56$ 220. $k < 3$

221. $x \le 6/5$ 222. $m \ge 5$ 223. $m \le 8$ 224. $m > 10$

225. $x \le 5$ 226. $k > 3$ 227. $z \ge -12$ 228. $x \le 5/2$

229. $z \le -1$ 230. $m < -2$ 231. $z \le -45$ 232. $y < -1$

233. $k \le 10$ 234. $m \ge 16$ 235. $k > 4$ 236. $z \le 4/3$

237. $x > 3$ 238. $k < -5/3$ 239. $y \le -1$ 240. $k < 5$

241. $k \le 1$ 242. $k \ge 40$ 243. $y \ge 3$ 244. $z \le 2/3$

245. $x \le 3$ 246. $m > -32$ 247. $y \le 15$ 248. $x \ge -4$

249. $m \le -1$ 250. $k \le -3/5$ 251. $x > -8$ 252. $y \le -6$

253. $y > -3$ 254. $y < 35$ 255. $z \ge -5$ 256. $k \le -11$

Page 35:   Verbal Algebra

257. 50	258. 2	259. 7	260. 0
261. 10	262. 4	263. 3, 4, 5, 6	264. 8, 9, 10
265. 6, 7, 8	266. 3	267. 11	268. 1, 2
269. 5	270. 80	271. 9	272. 6, 7
273. 36	274. 18	275. 3	276. 6
277. 10	278. 2	279. 17	280. 6
281. 1, 2, 3	282. 1, 4	283. 9	284. 8
285. 7	286. 11	287. 9	288. 3
289. 10	290. 4, 5	291. 1	292. 36
293. 12	294. 1, 2, 3, 4	295. 3	296. 4, 36
297. 8			

Page 43: Linear Equations

1. -9	11. -5	21. -1
2. 4	12. -4	22. -2
3. -2	13. 8	23. 0
4. -7	14. -5	24. 0
5. 5	15. 9	25. -3
6. -2	16. 1	26. 2
7. -8	17. 1	27. 8
8. -8	18. 3	28. 1
9. -4	19. 2	29. -2
10. 9	20. 5	30. -7

Page 47: Find Slope from Two Points

1. 3	11. 10	21. 2
2. 9	12. -8	22. 1
3. -2	13. -3	23. -9
4. -6	14. -4	24. 10
5. 0	15. -8	25. 9
6. -3	16. 0	26. 6
7. 0	17. -2	27. -5
8. 10	18. 0	28. 0
9. 3	19. 5	29. 7
10. 4	20. 2	30. -5

Page 51: Quadratic Equations

1. -1.378, 2.178	21. 2.553, -0.839	41. -4.899, 4.899
2. No solution.	22. No solution.	42. 17, -7
3. -1.944, 2.444	23. 0.957, -0.957	43. -5, 4.333
4. -2, 3	24. -1.333, 4	44. -12, 12
5. -2.55, 2.55	25. -5, 5	45. -1.281, 0.781
6. No solution.	26. -2, -3	46. -4, 2.25
7. No solution.	27. -0.894, 0.894	47. -2, -3
8. -4.5, 7.5	28. -0.163, 0.877	48. 1.359, -7.359
9. -1, -1.25	29. 5.5, -3.5	49. -1.118, 1.118
10. 2, -1.167	30. -1.228, 0.592	50. 0.956, -1.831
11. 1.414, -1.414	31. -0.459, -6.541	51. 0.099, -0.917
12. 1.618, -0.618	32. No solution.	52. -6, 6
13. -0.687, 1.323	33. 5, -1.333	53. -9, 13
14. No solution.	34. 0.769, -4.769	54. 6, -2
15. 1.095, -0.761	35. -4, 10	55. 1.446, -1.446
16. 0.2, -1	36. 4.333, -2	56. -1.77, 0.77
17. 0.647, -0.772	37. No solution.	57. 5.5, -5.5
18. 4.5, -5	38. 1, -2.167	58. No solution.
19. 0.089, 1.411	39. No solution.	59. 1.456, -2.289
20. -2, -1	40. -1.5, 1.5	60. 6.887, -1.887